Remembering WOMEN ARTISTS

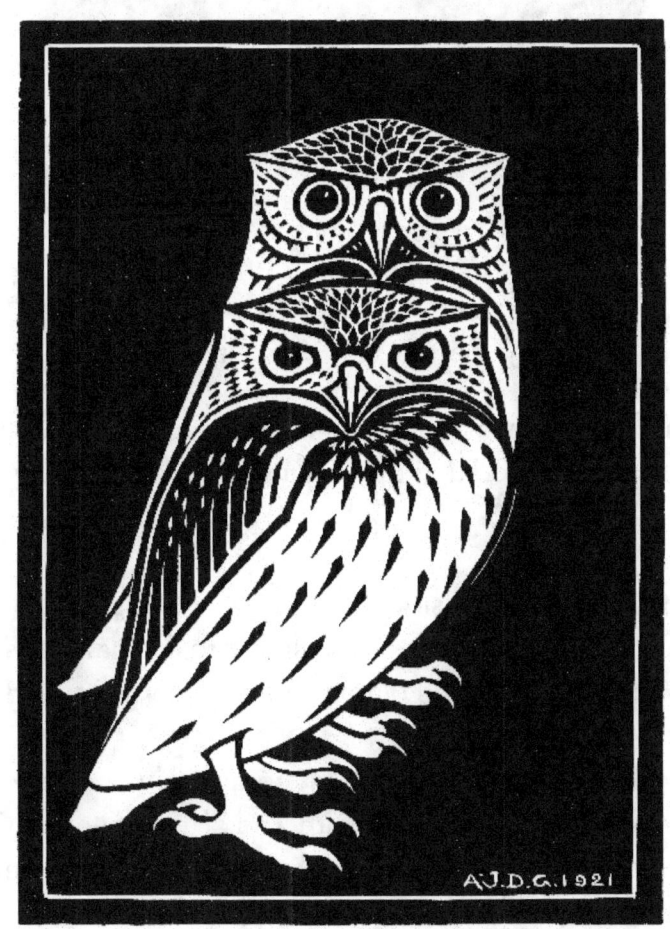

Julie de Graag

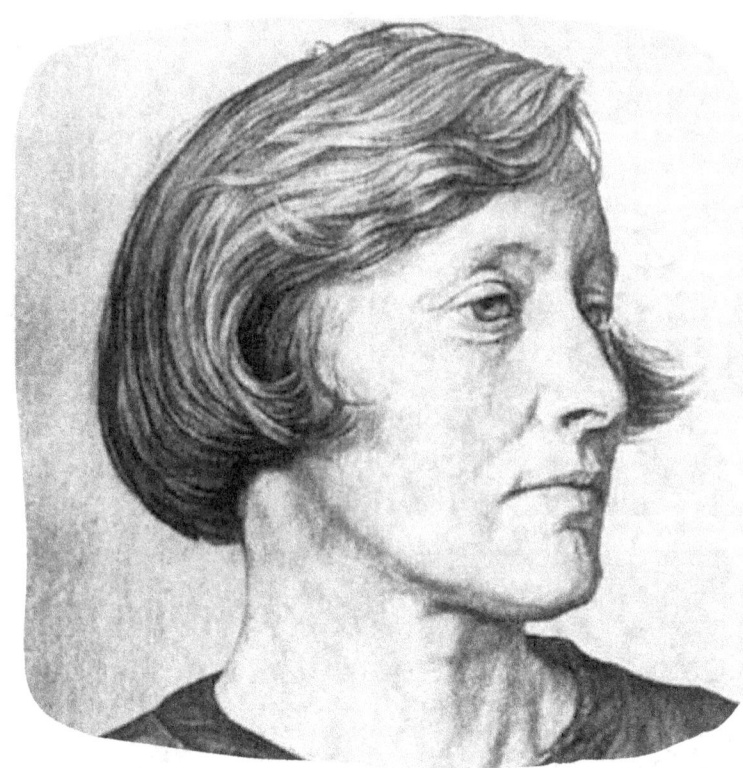

Portrait of Julie de Graag
by Bertha van Hasselt

Julie de Graag was born in Gorinchem, in southern Holland in 1877. She studied at the Hague in 1890 and earned her certificate. In addition to working as an artist, she gave taught drawing at a girls' school in Utrecht.

Julie de Graag primarily made woodcuts using the end grain, as opposed to the more common longitudinal wood grain. This method is more difficult due to the hardness of the wood but allows for finer detail. Her subjects included plants, animals, portraits, and village views.

She faced many challenges. Her home burned down completely on New Year's Eve 1908, much of her work was lost. She was of fragile health and often stayed with her parents. In the early 1920s, she experienced challenges to both her physical and mental health. She needed to stop teaching. As a result of these challenges, the themes of her work became increasingly morbid.

She committed suicide at the age of 46.

Copyright © 2021 by Kymba Nijuck All rights reserved. No part of this publication may be reproduced, distributed, or transmitted in any form or by any means, including photocopying, recording, or other electronic or mechanical methods. www.ChurchOf.Art

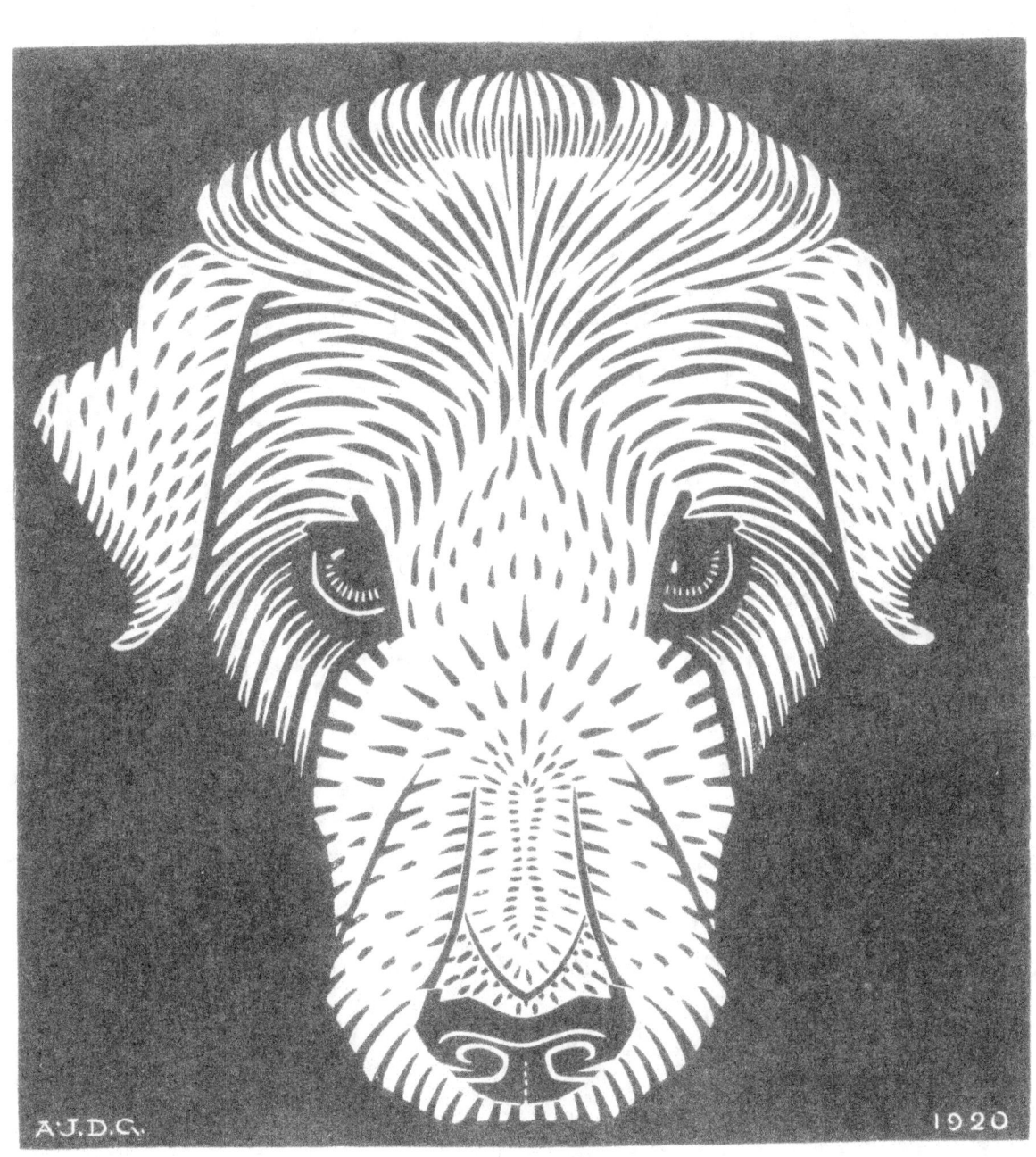

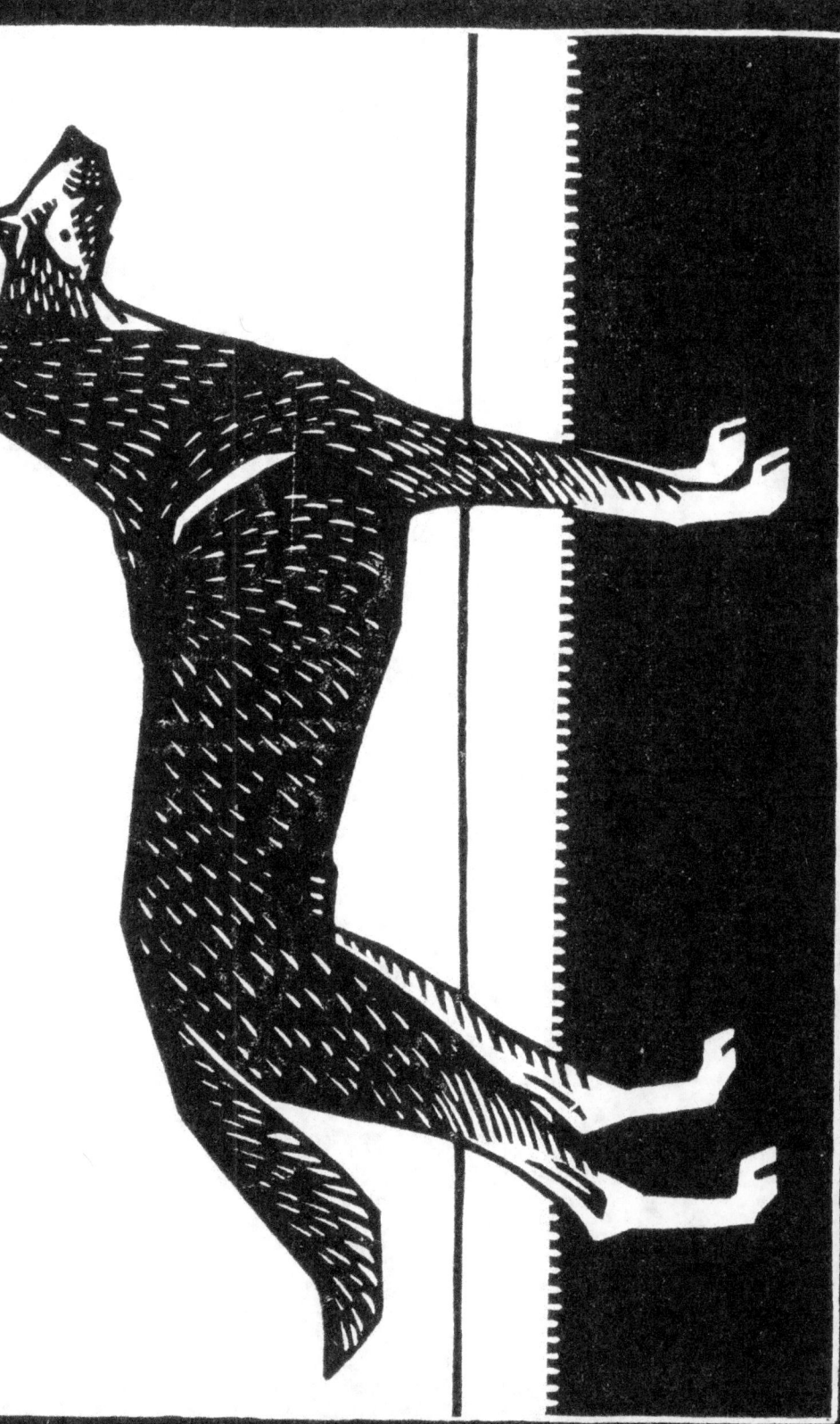

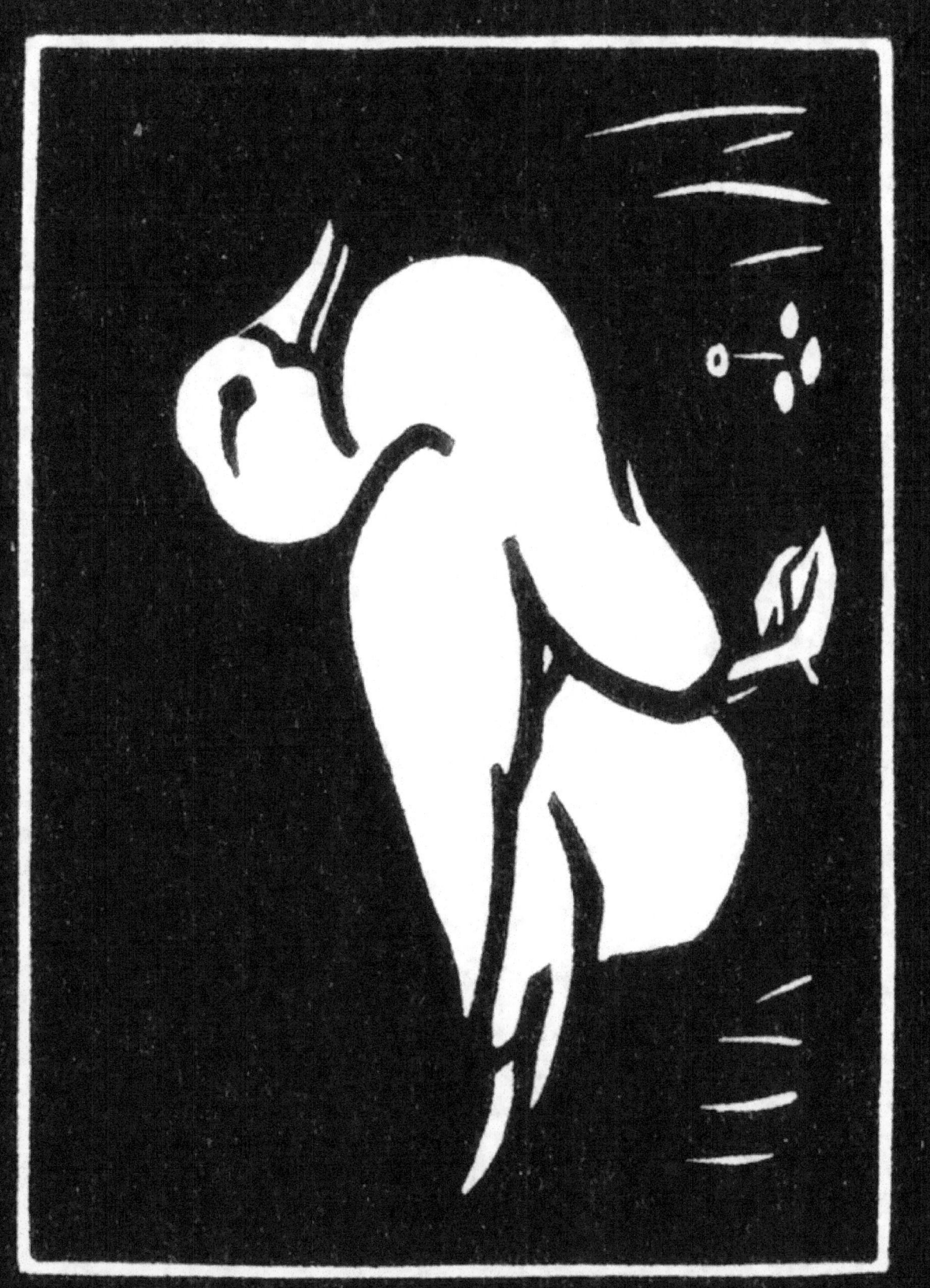

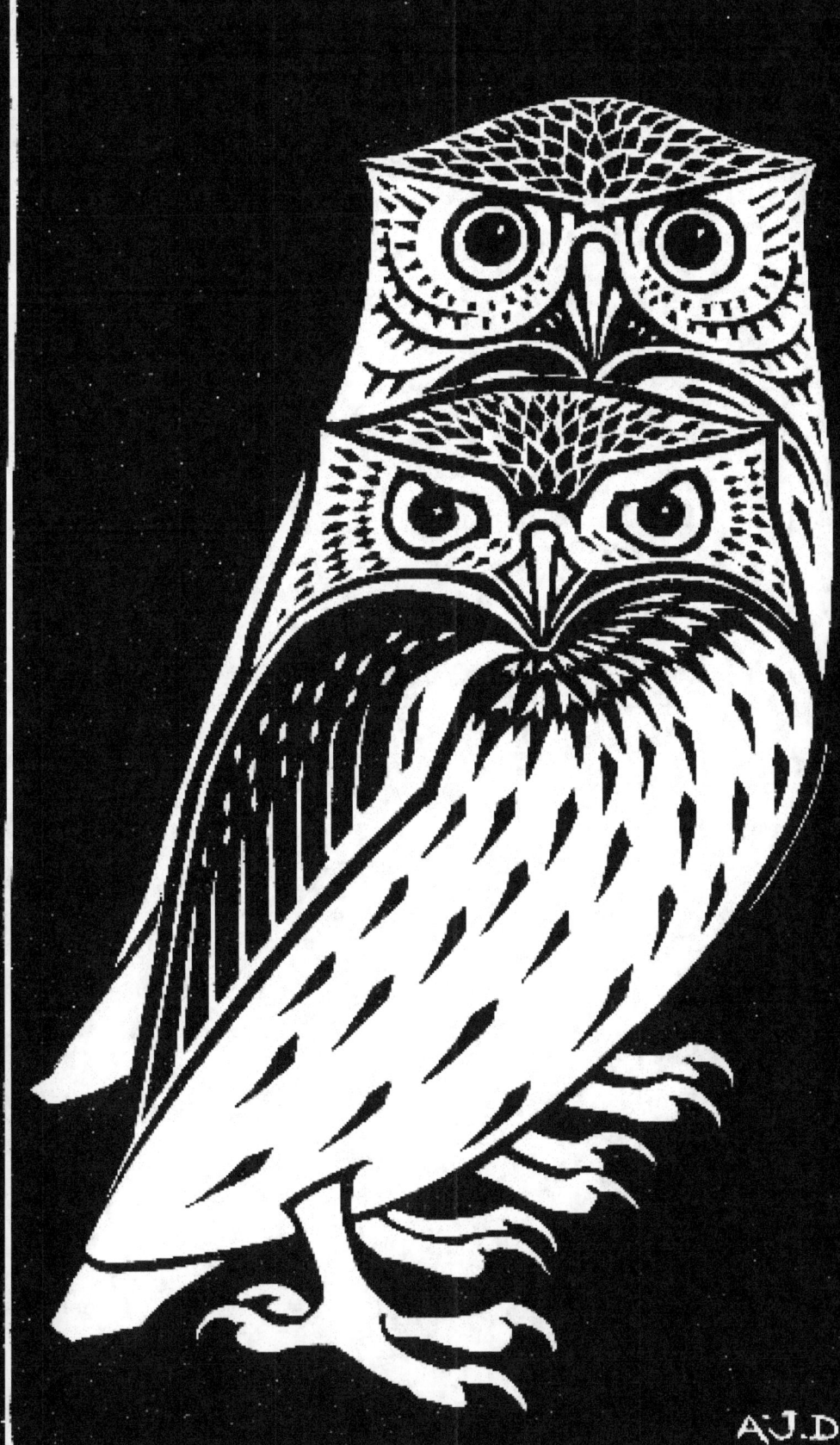

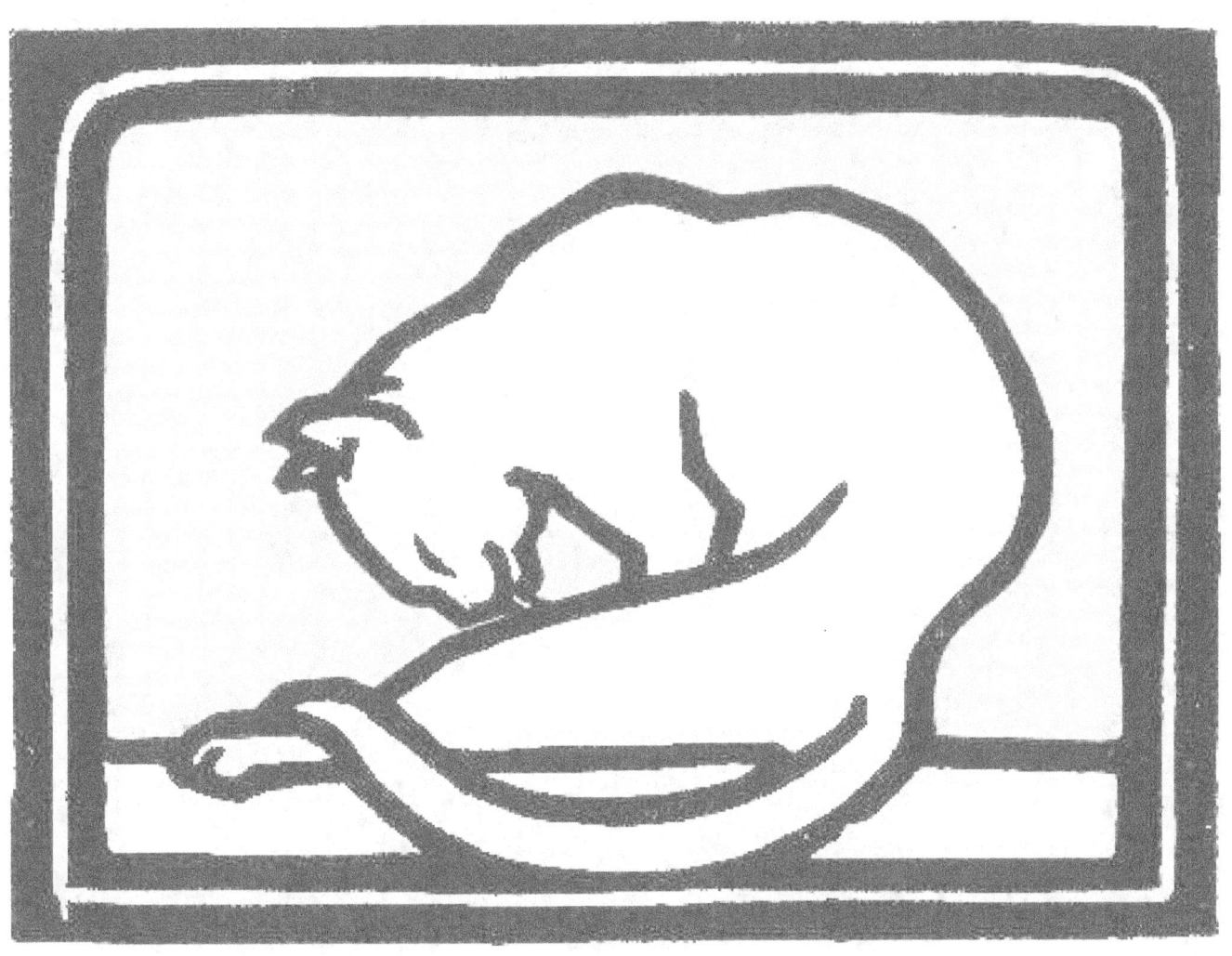

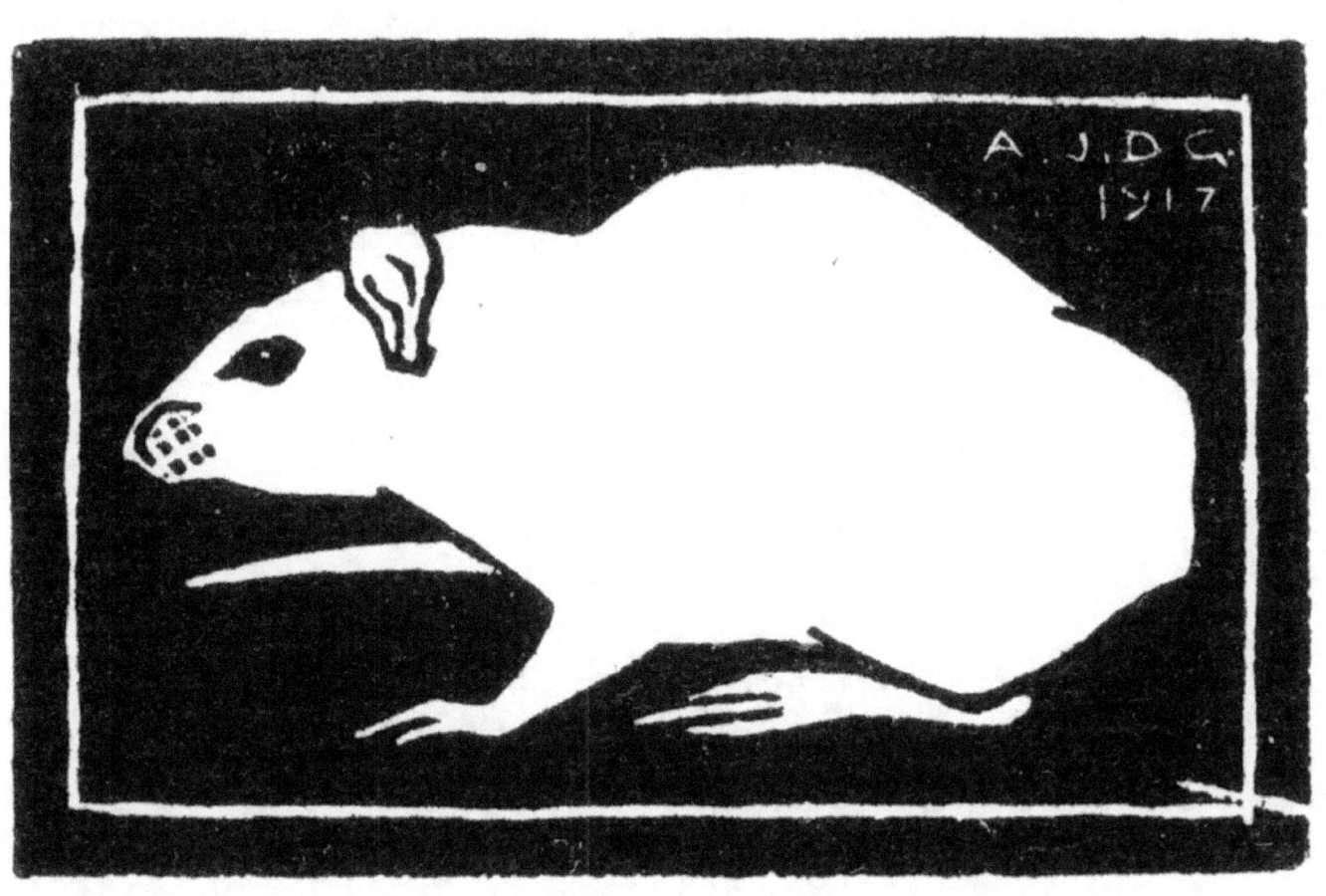

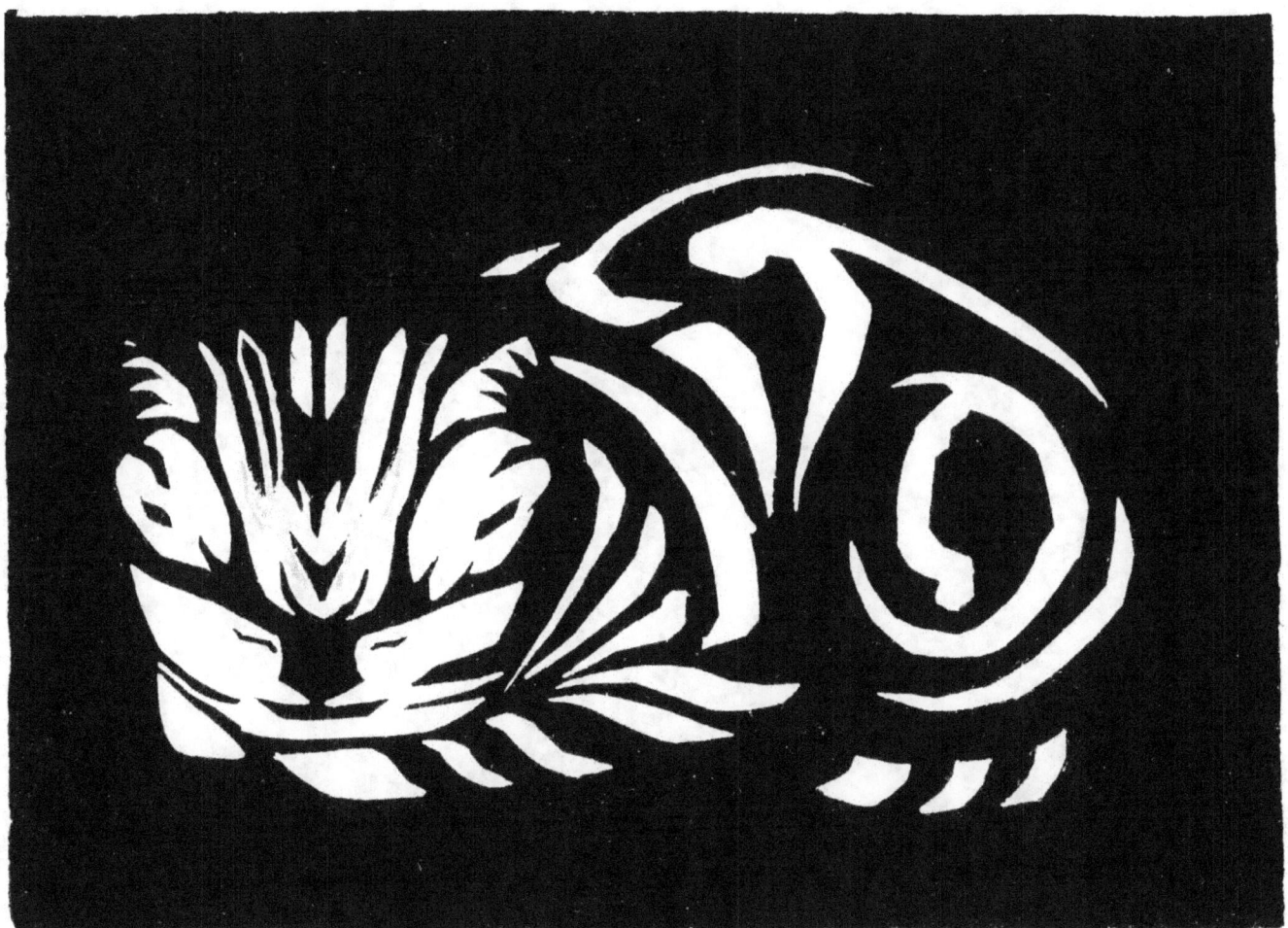

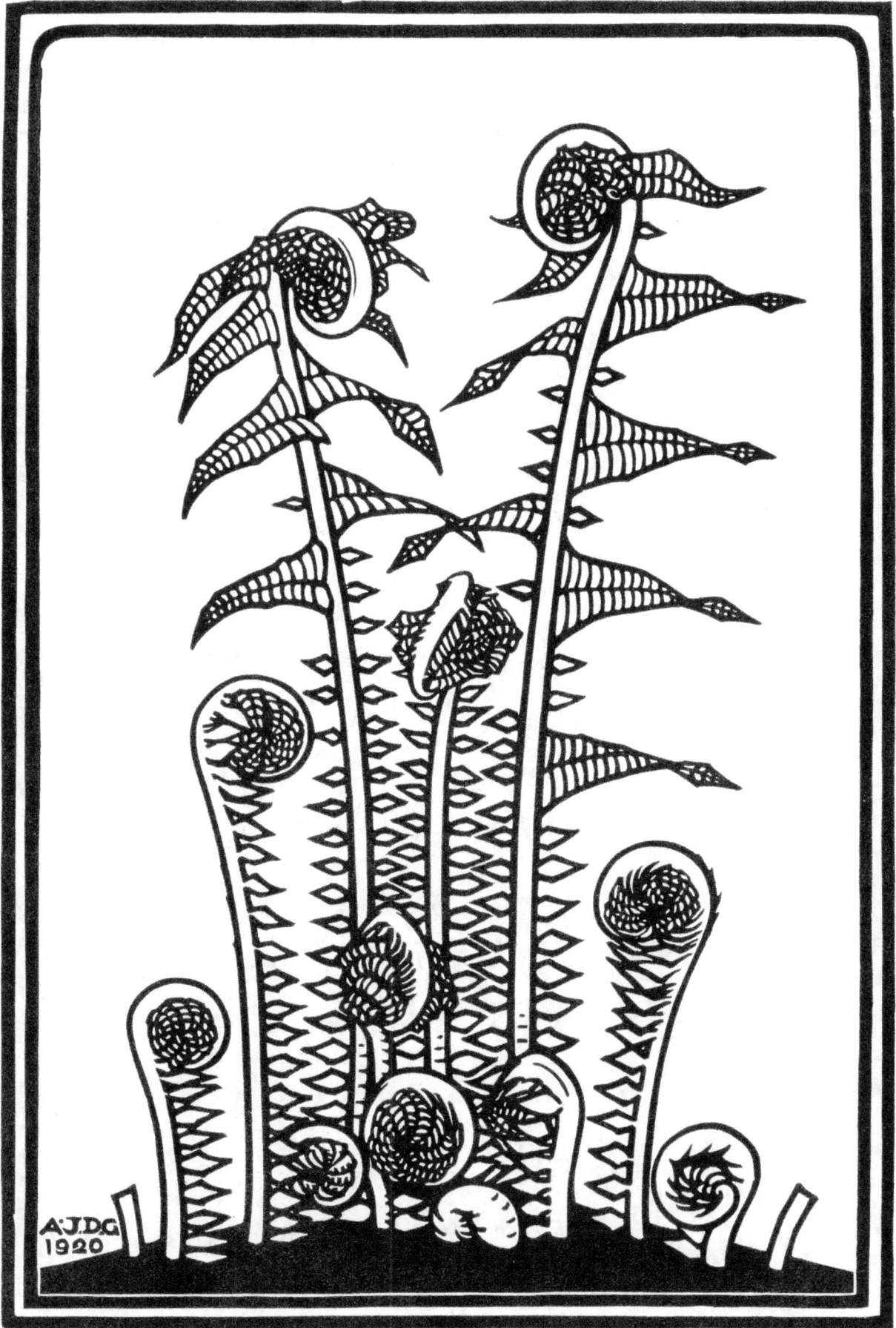

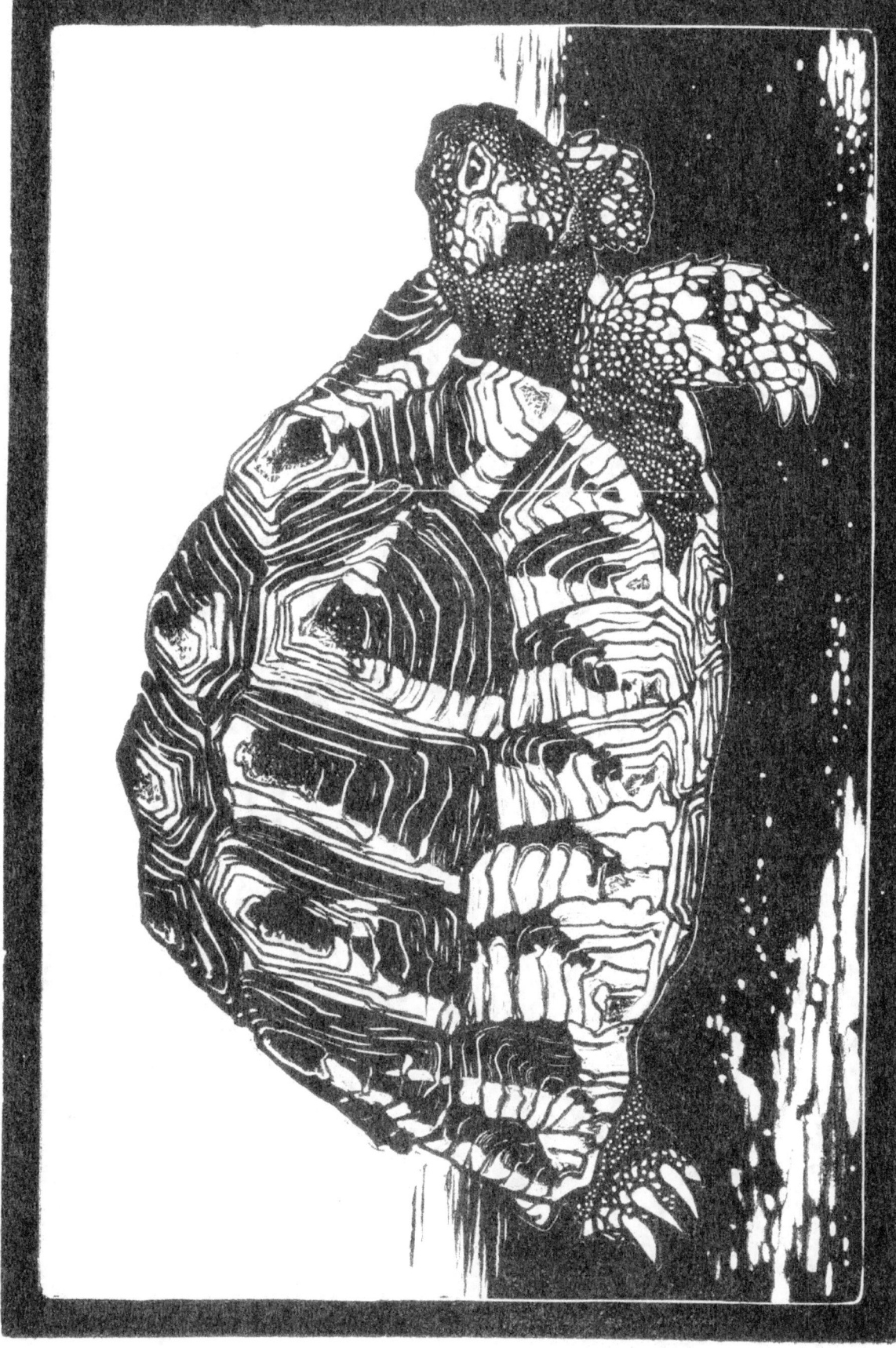

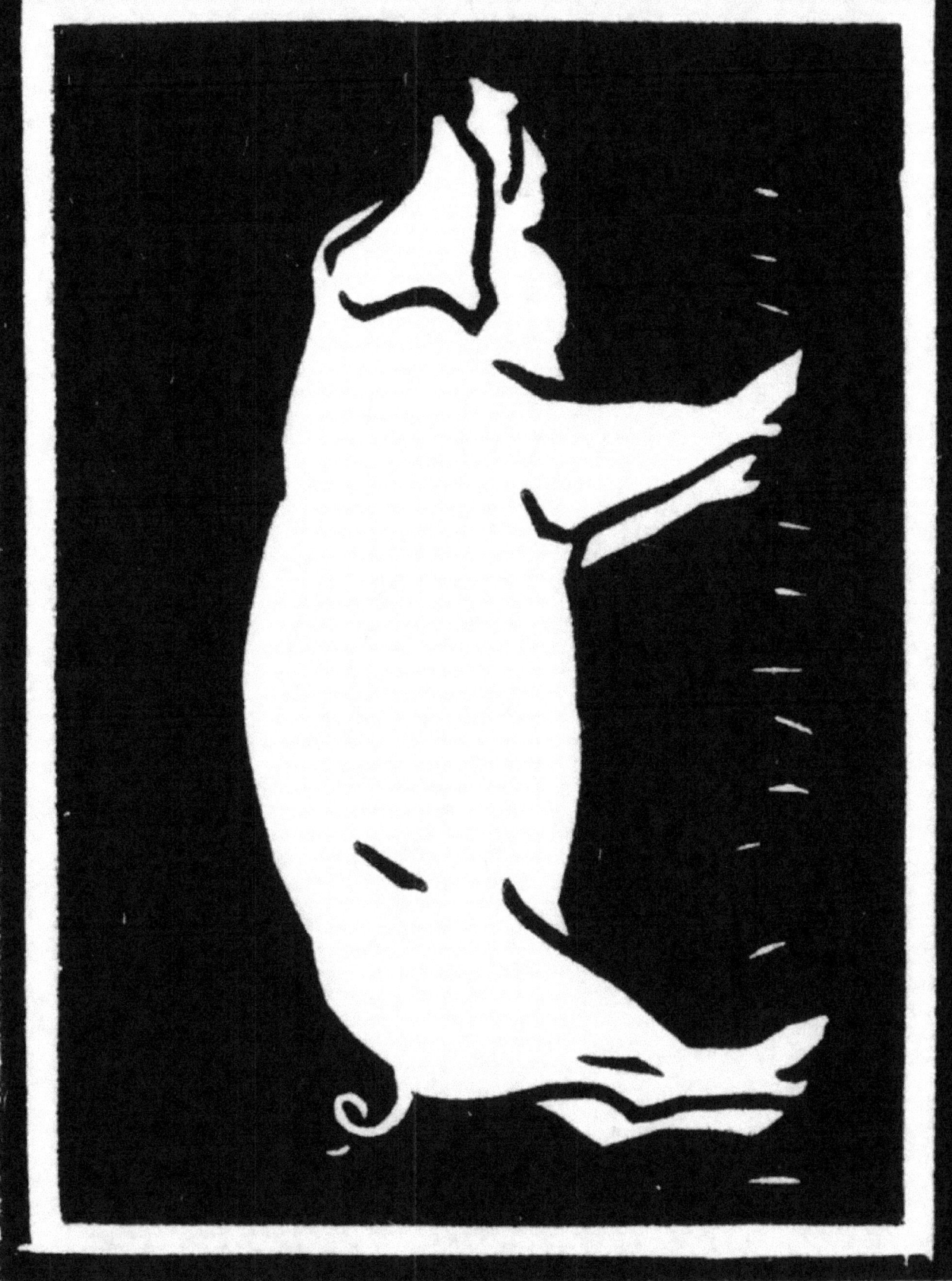

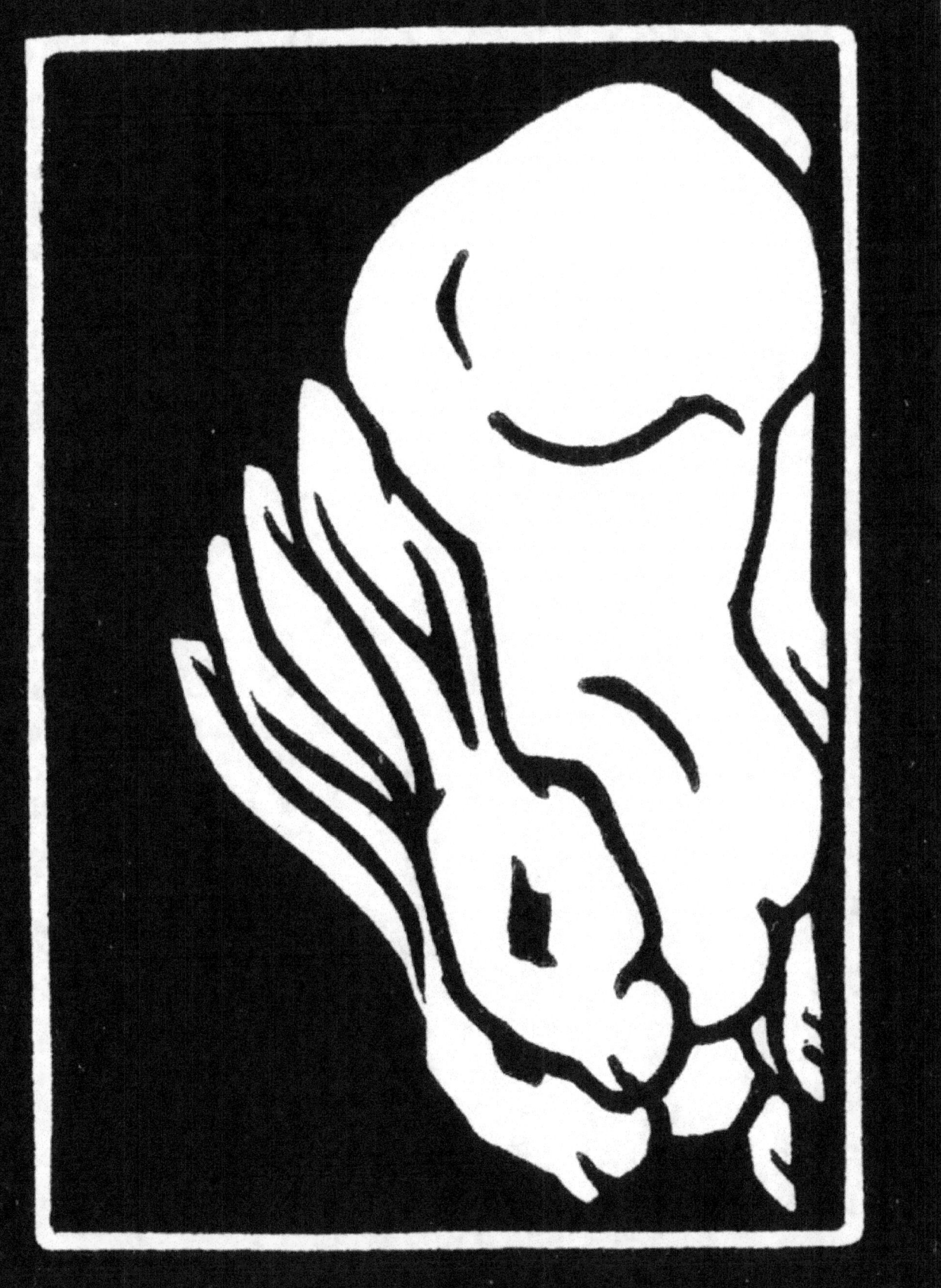

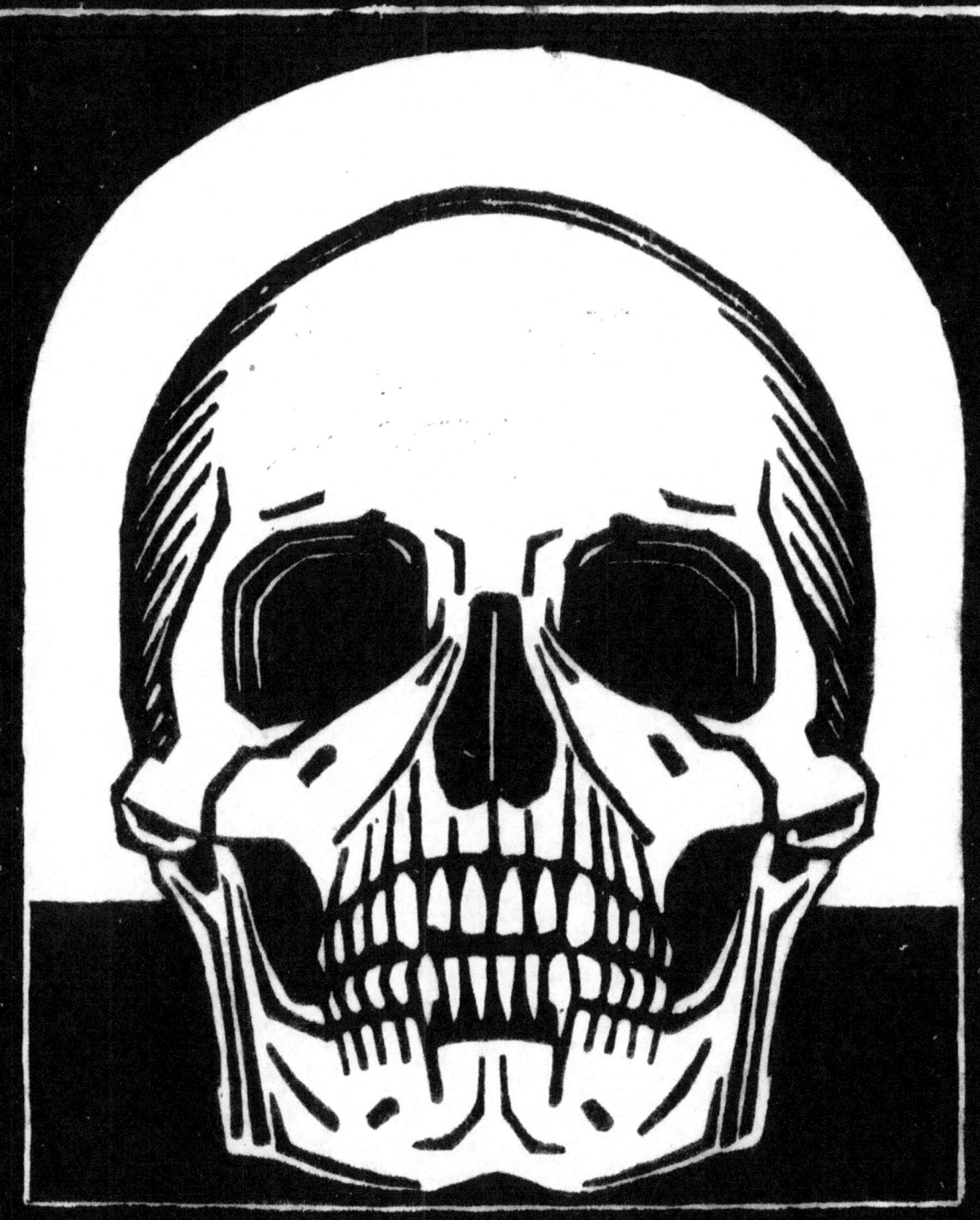

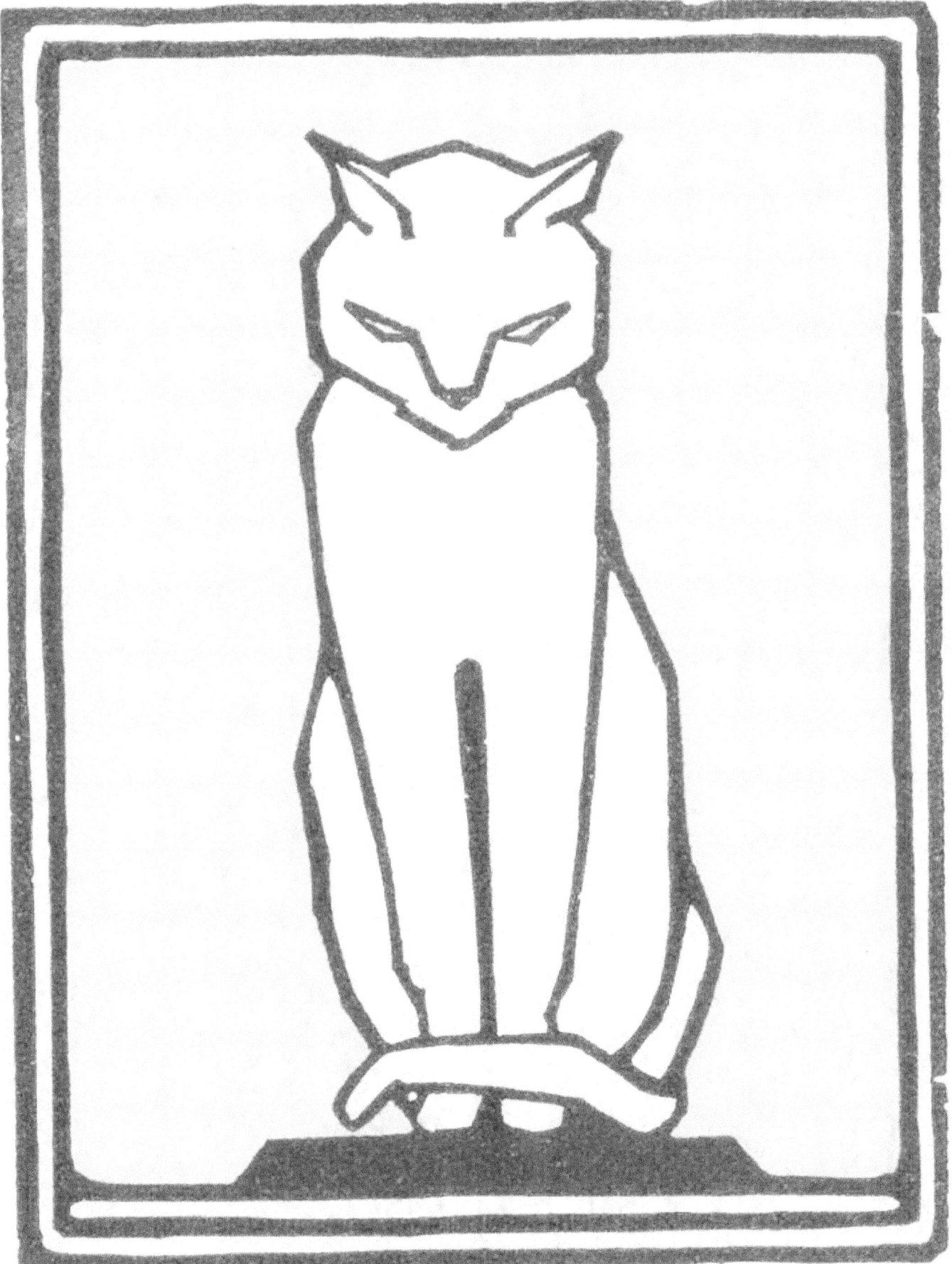

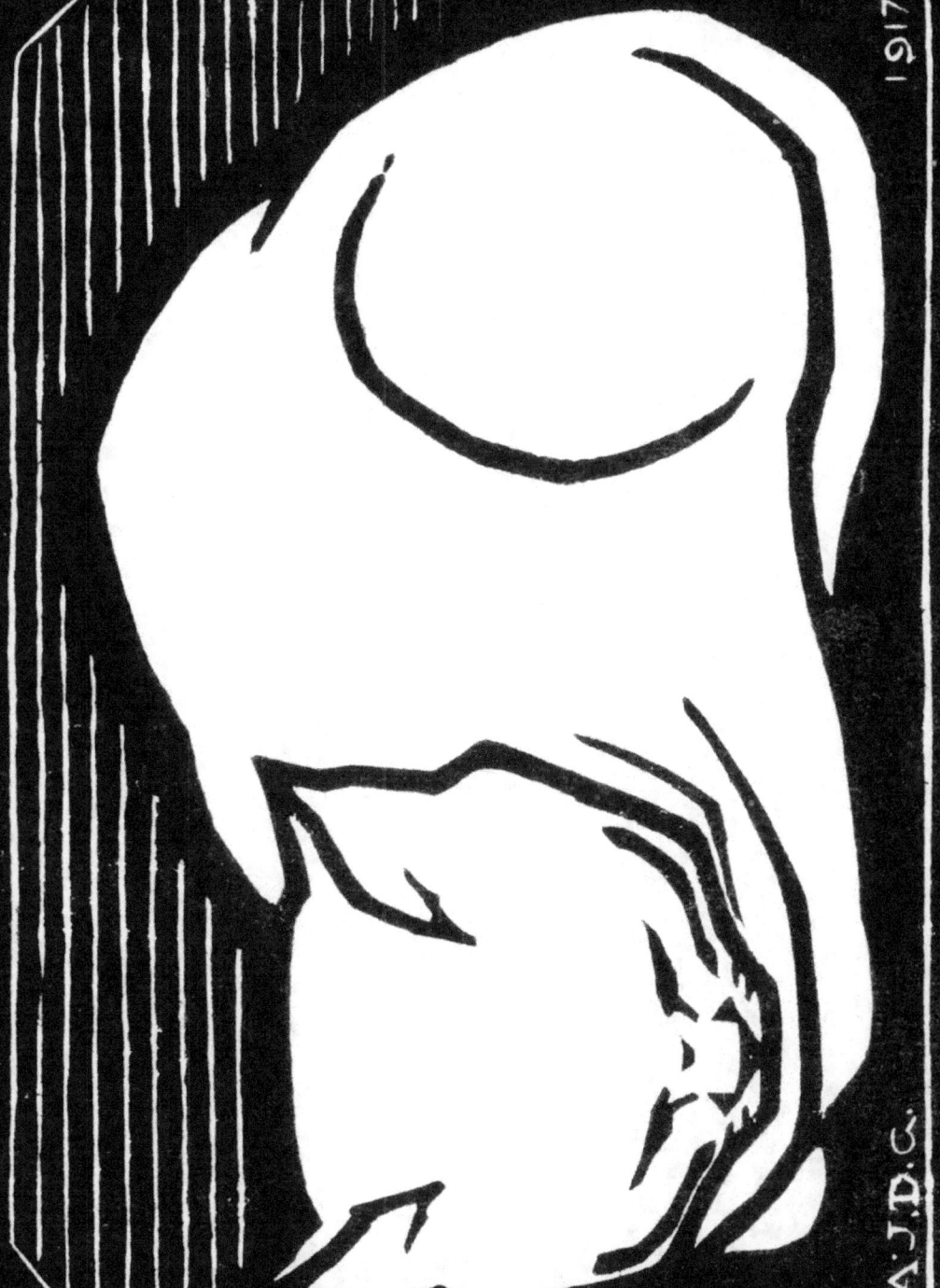

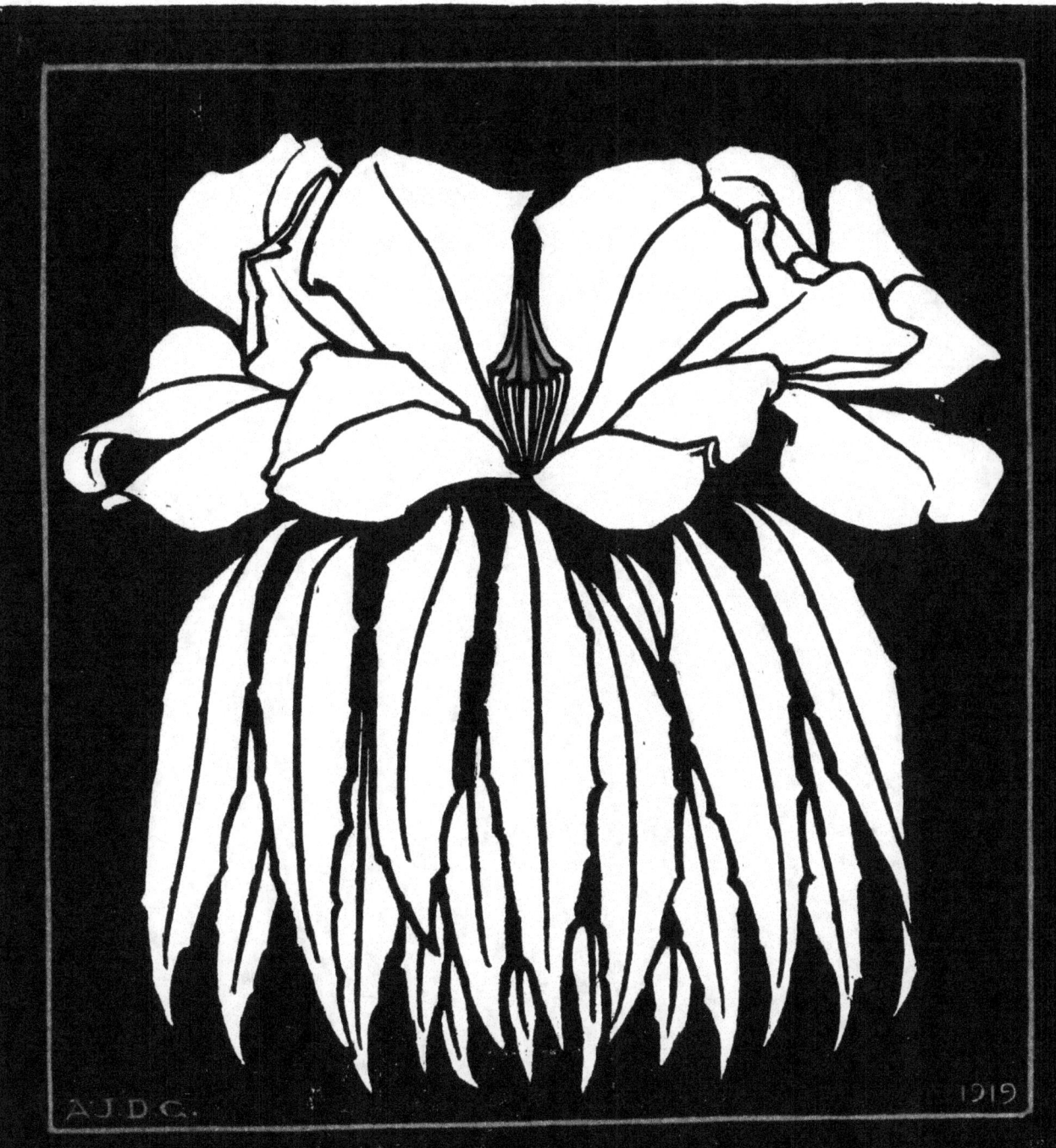

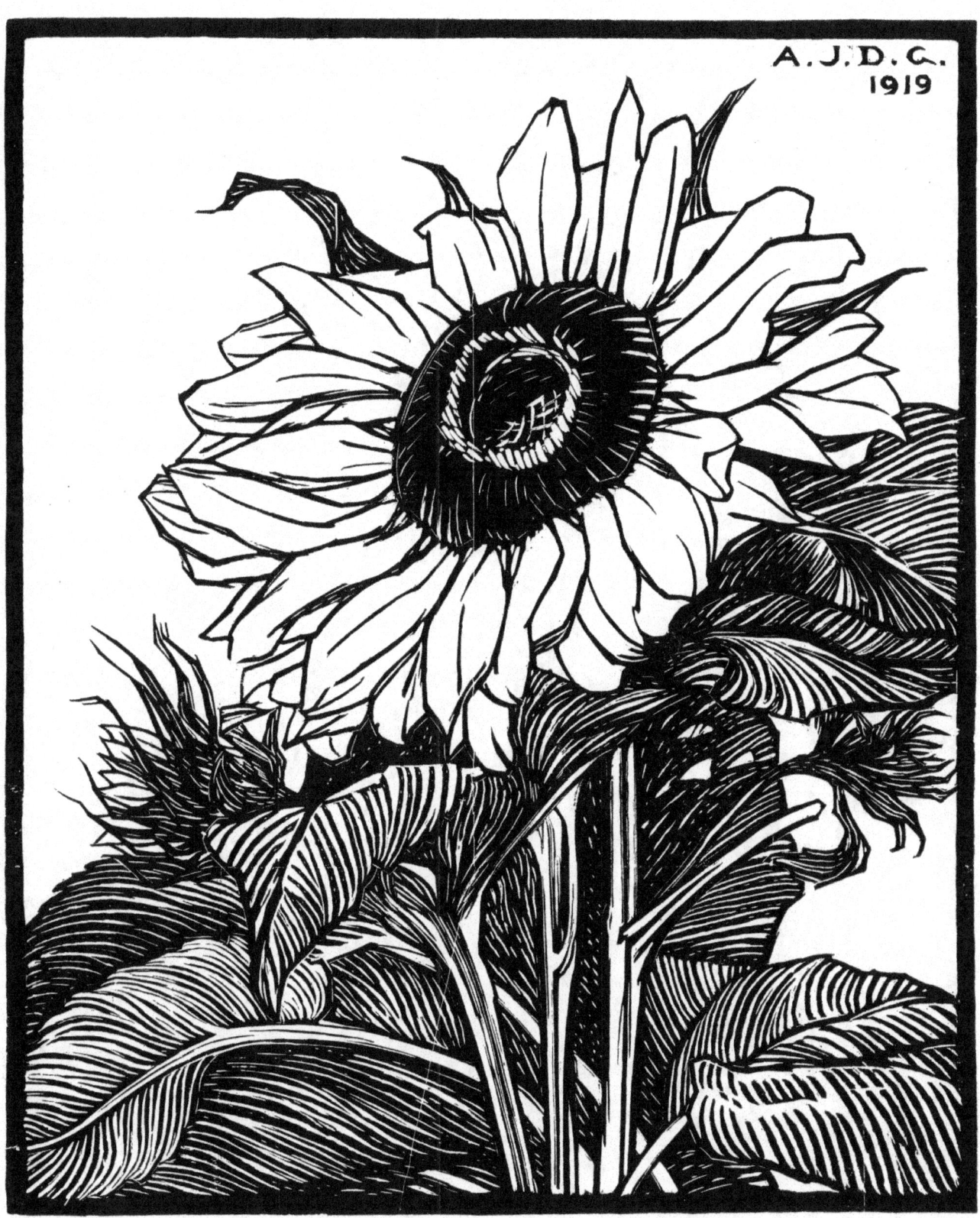

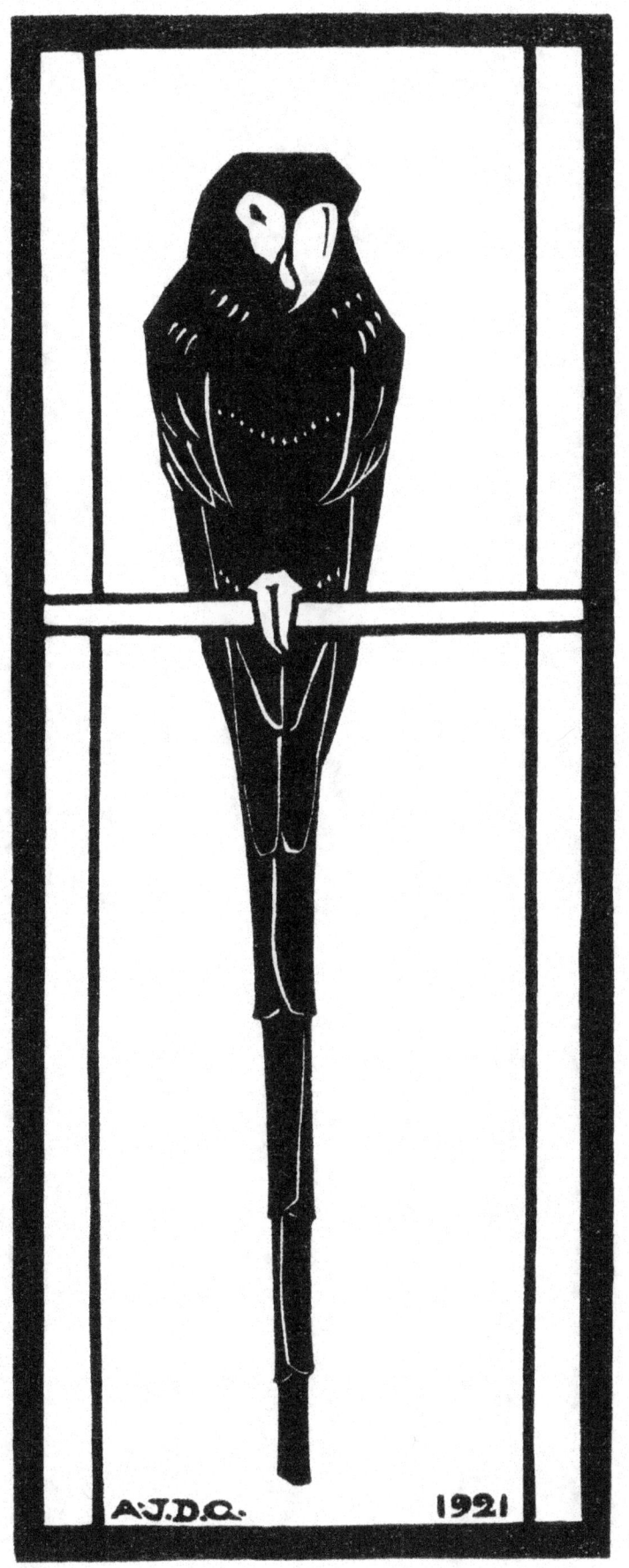

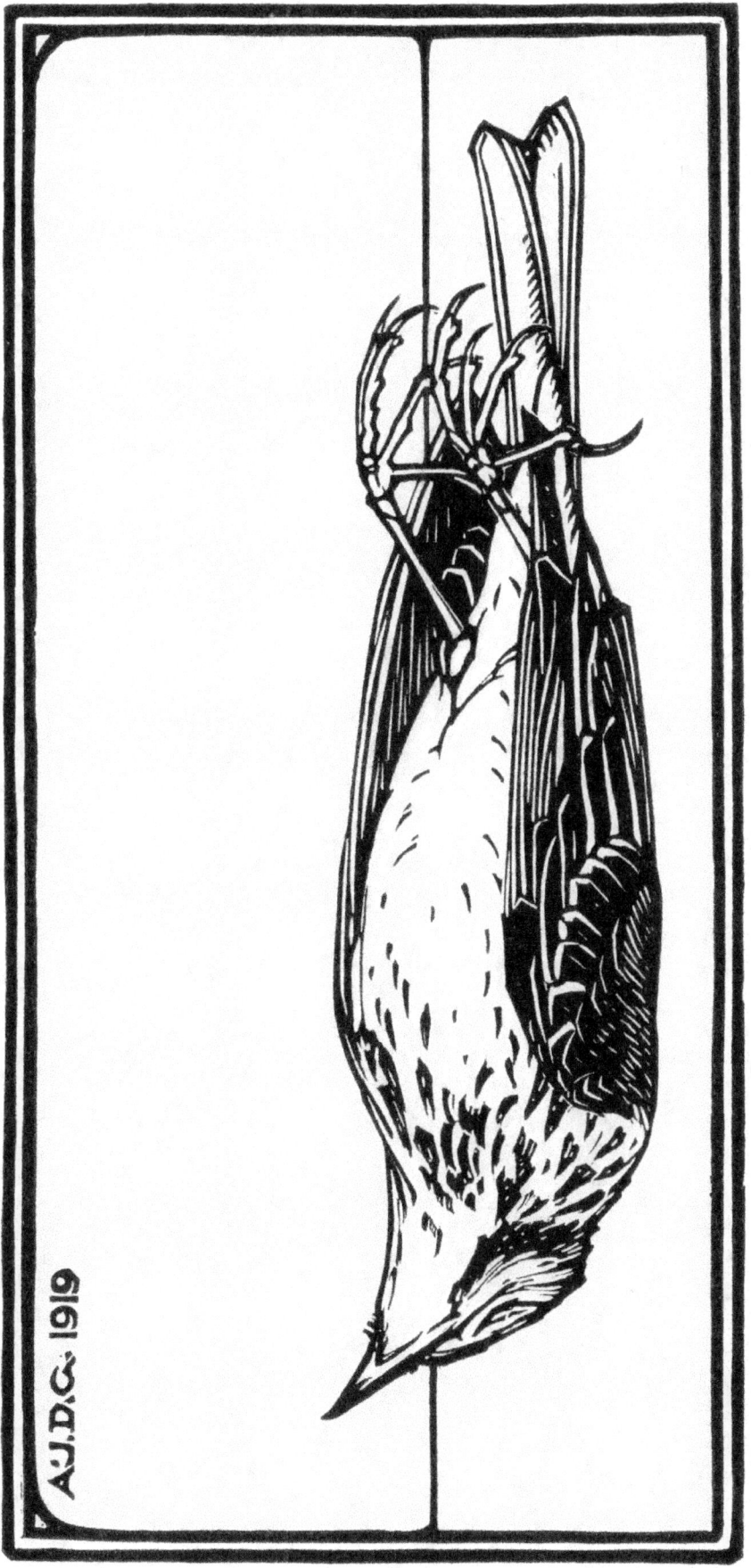

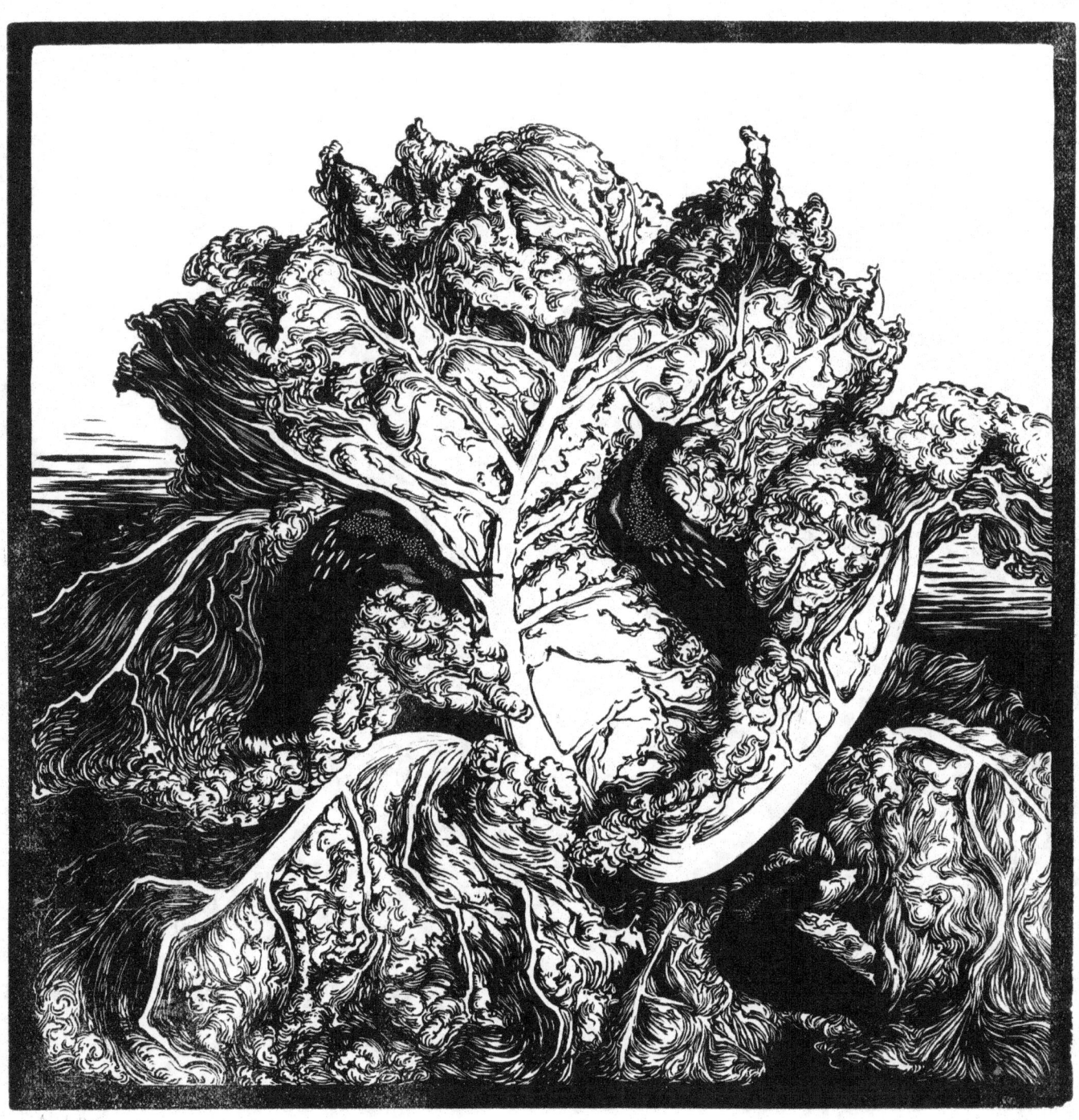

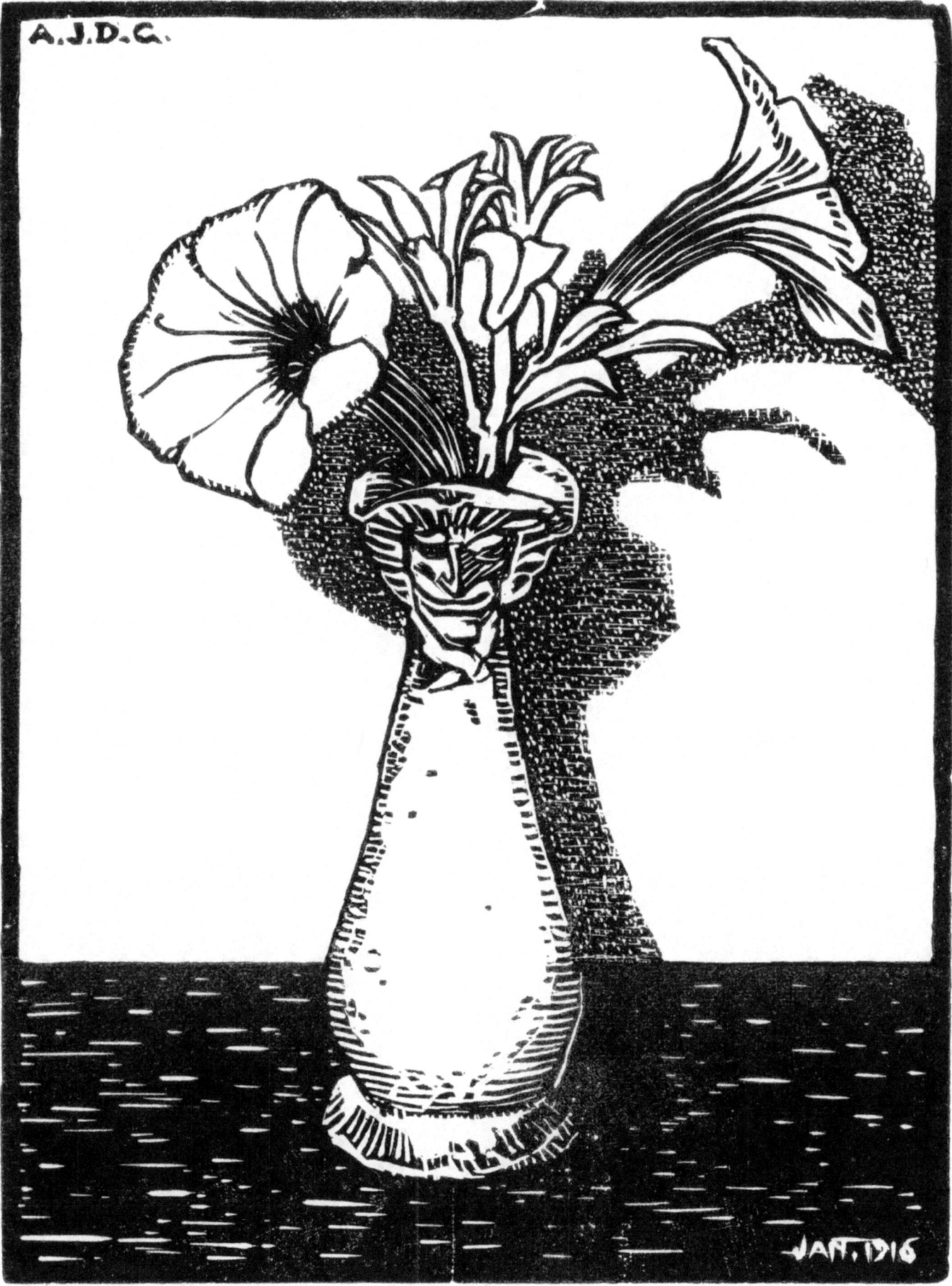

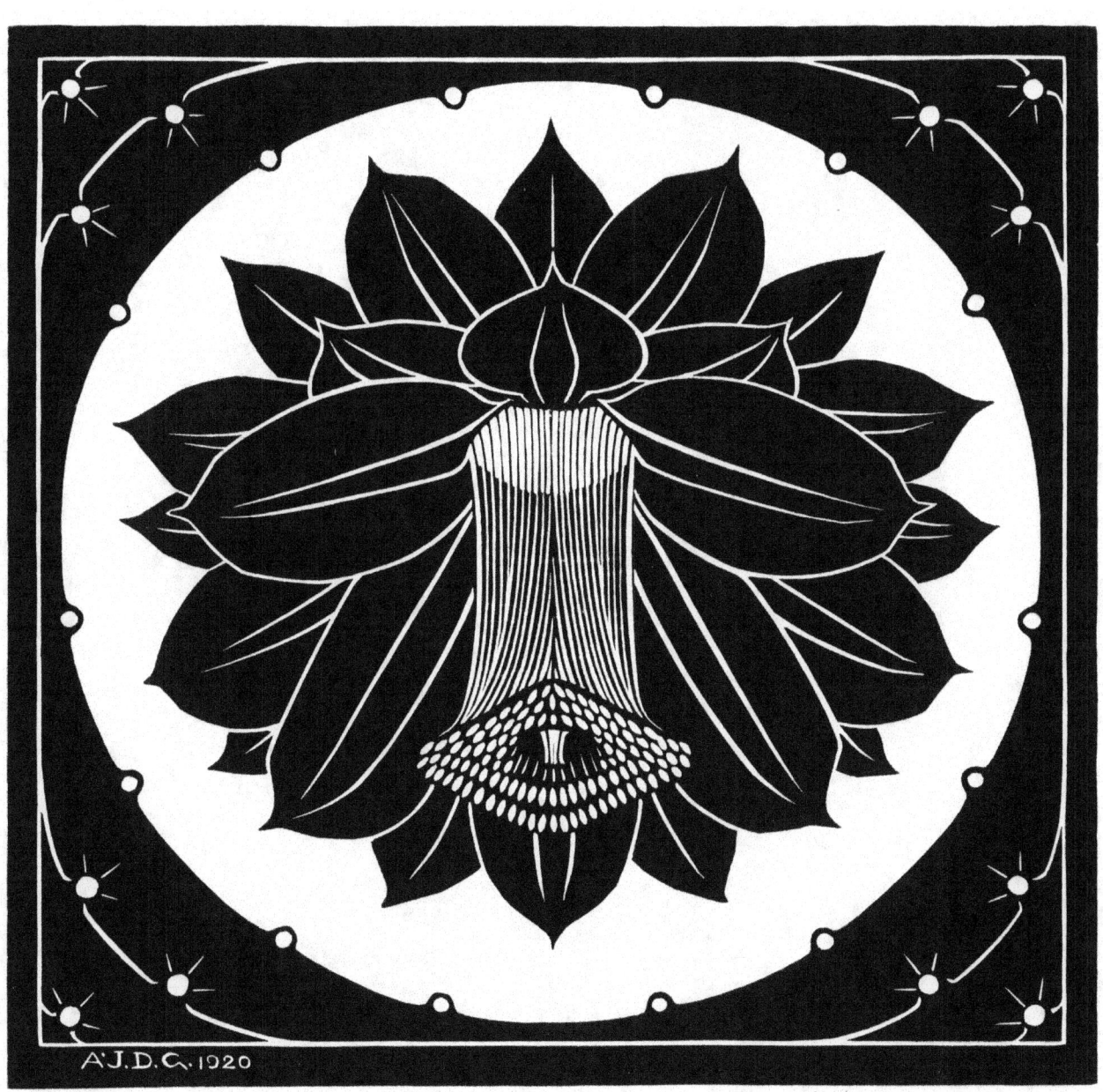

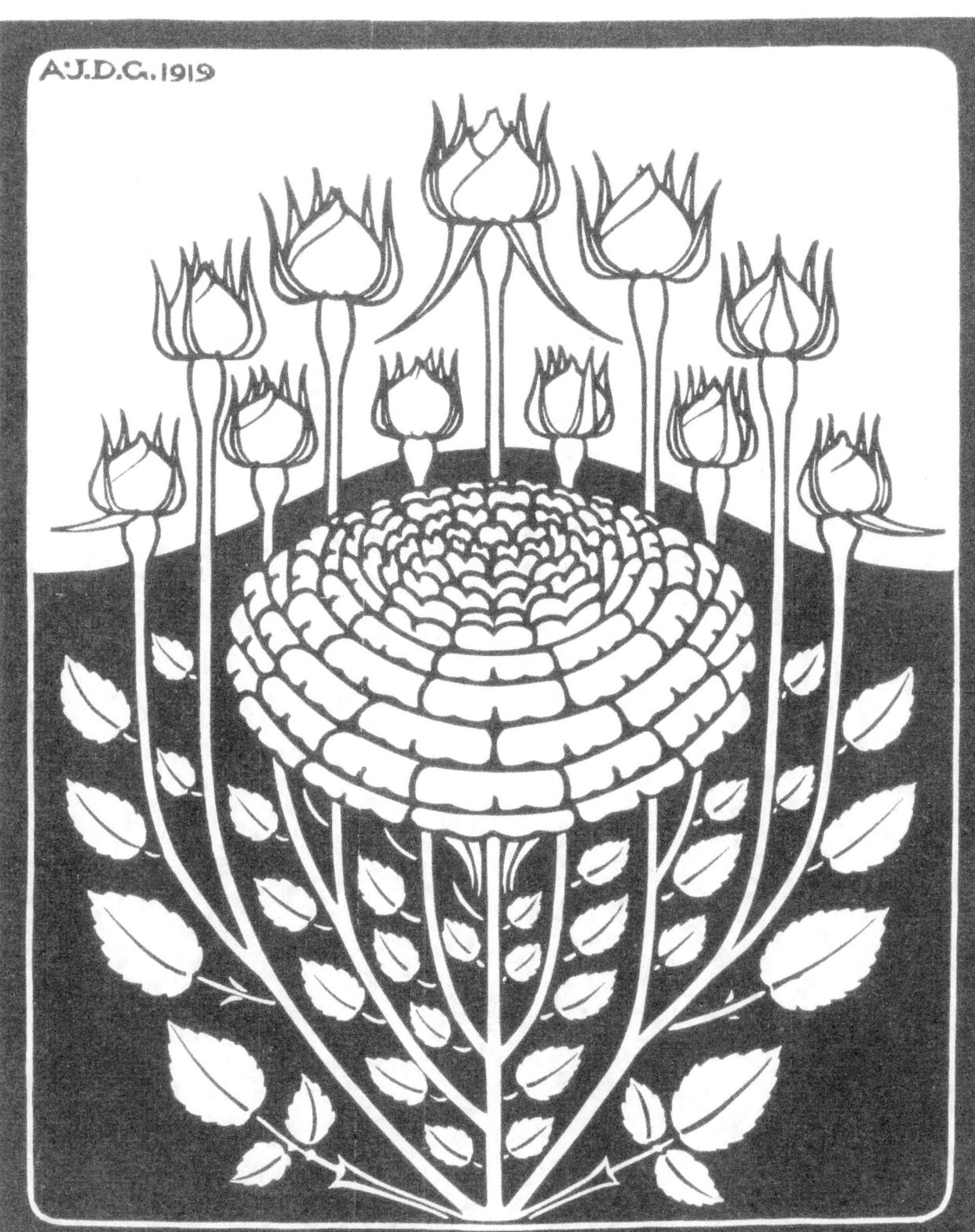

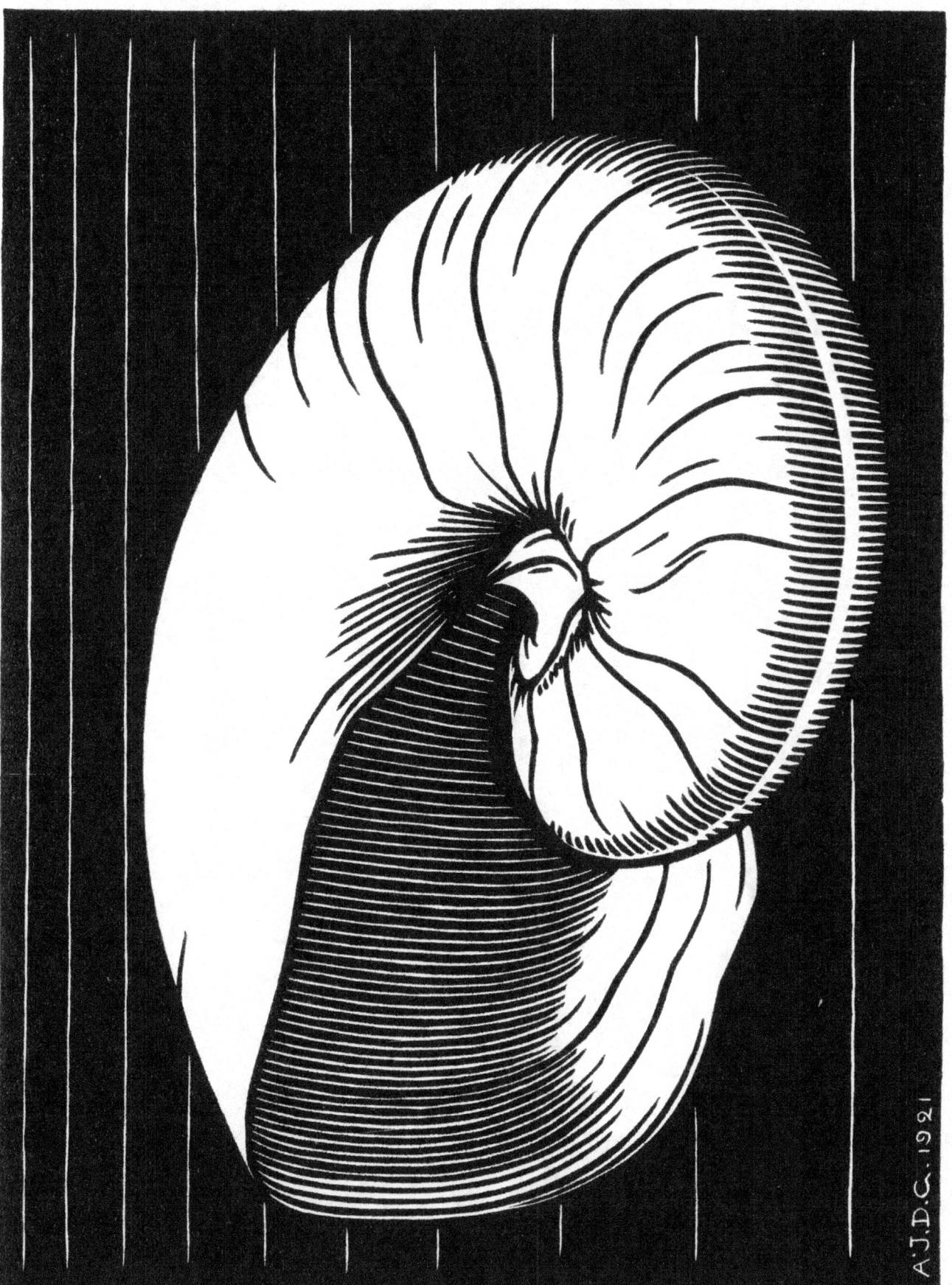

1916 VOOR ELSJE A.J.D.G.

MAX POES AKBAR

MAART A.J.D.C. 1918 AKELEI

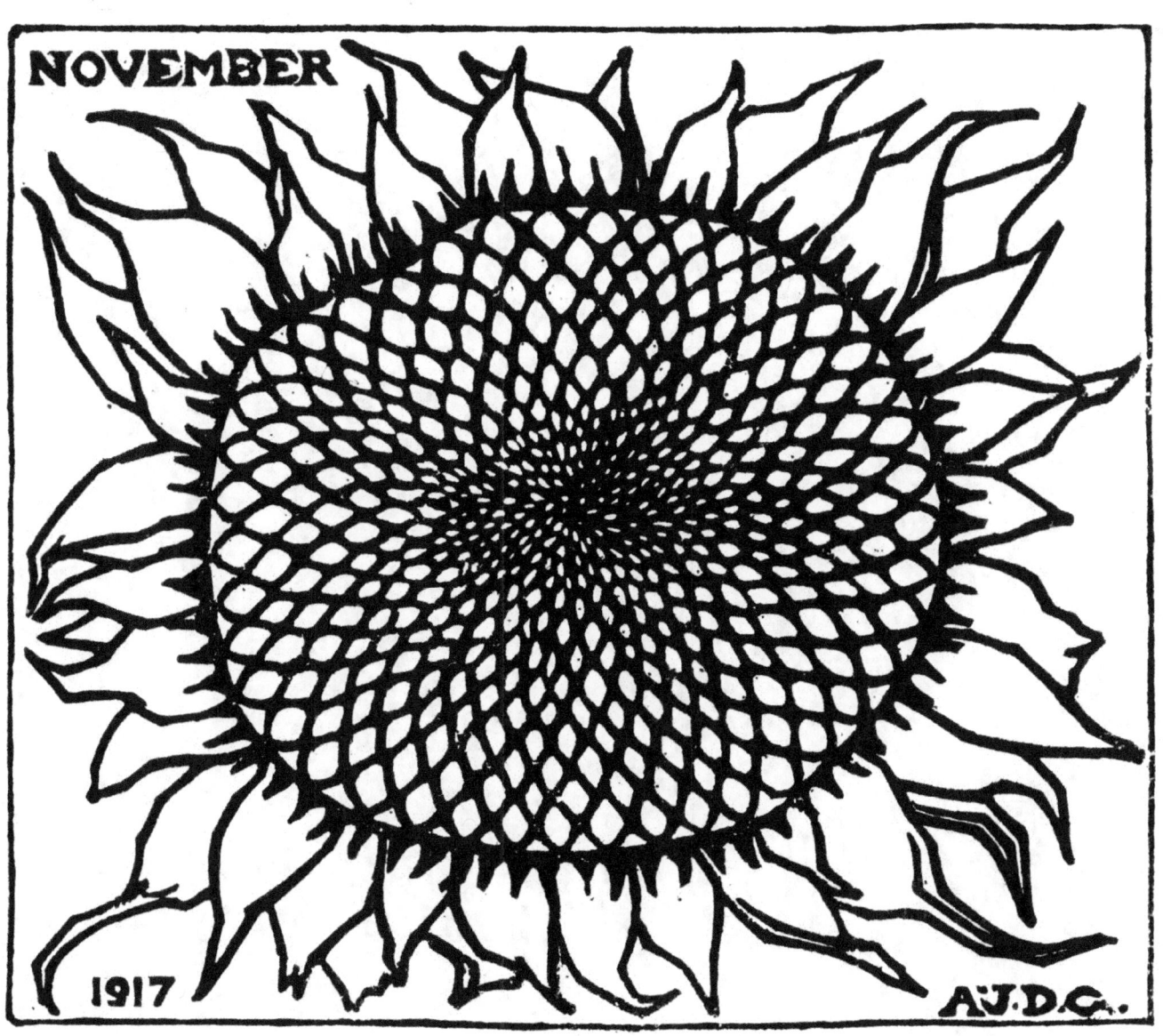

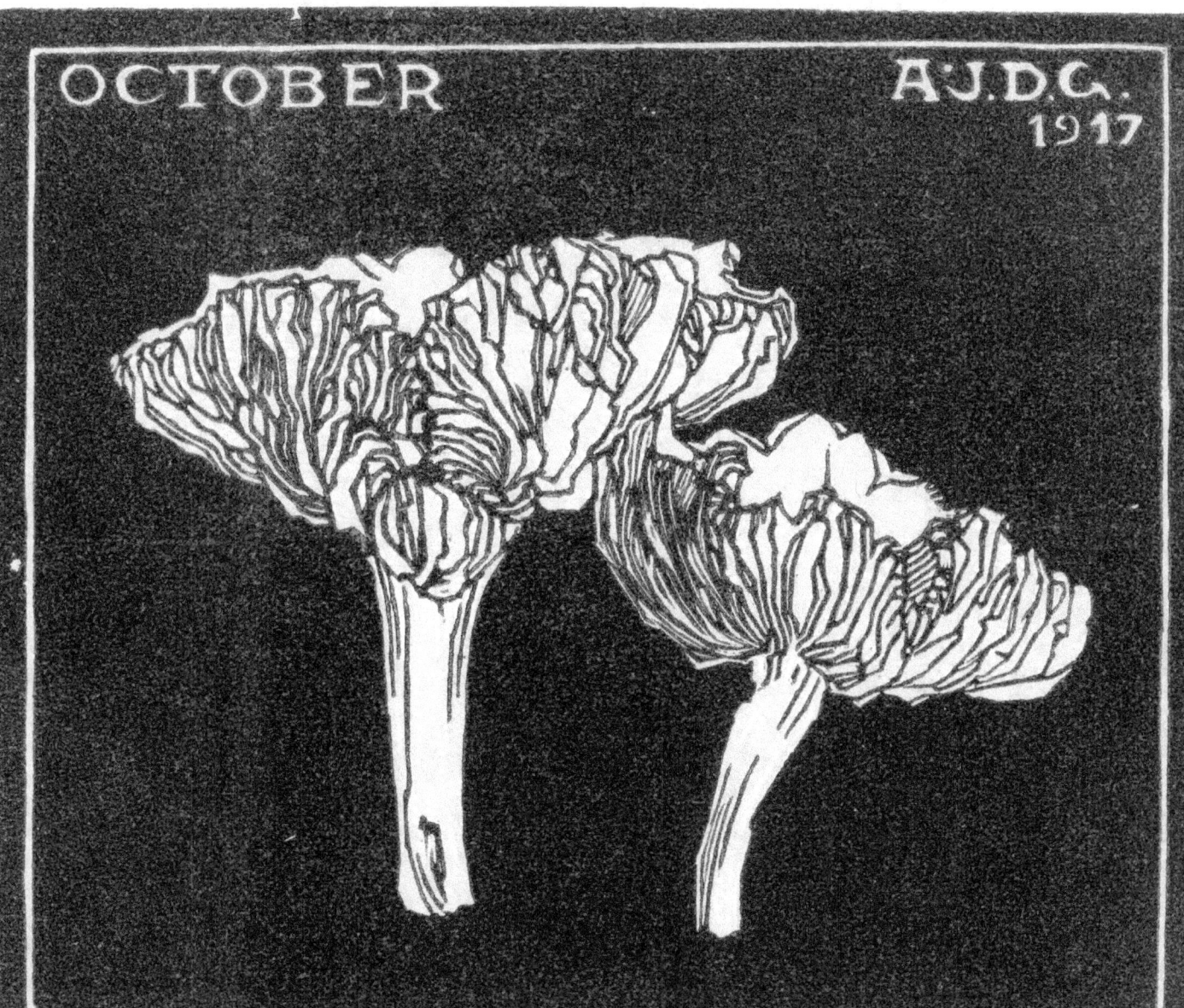

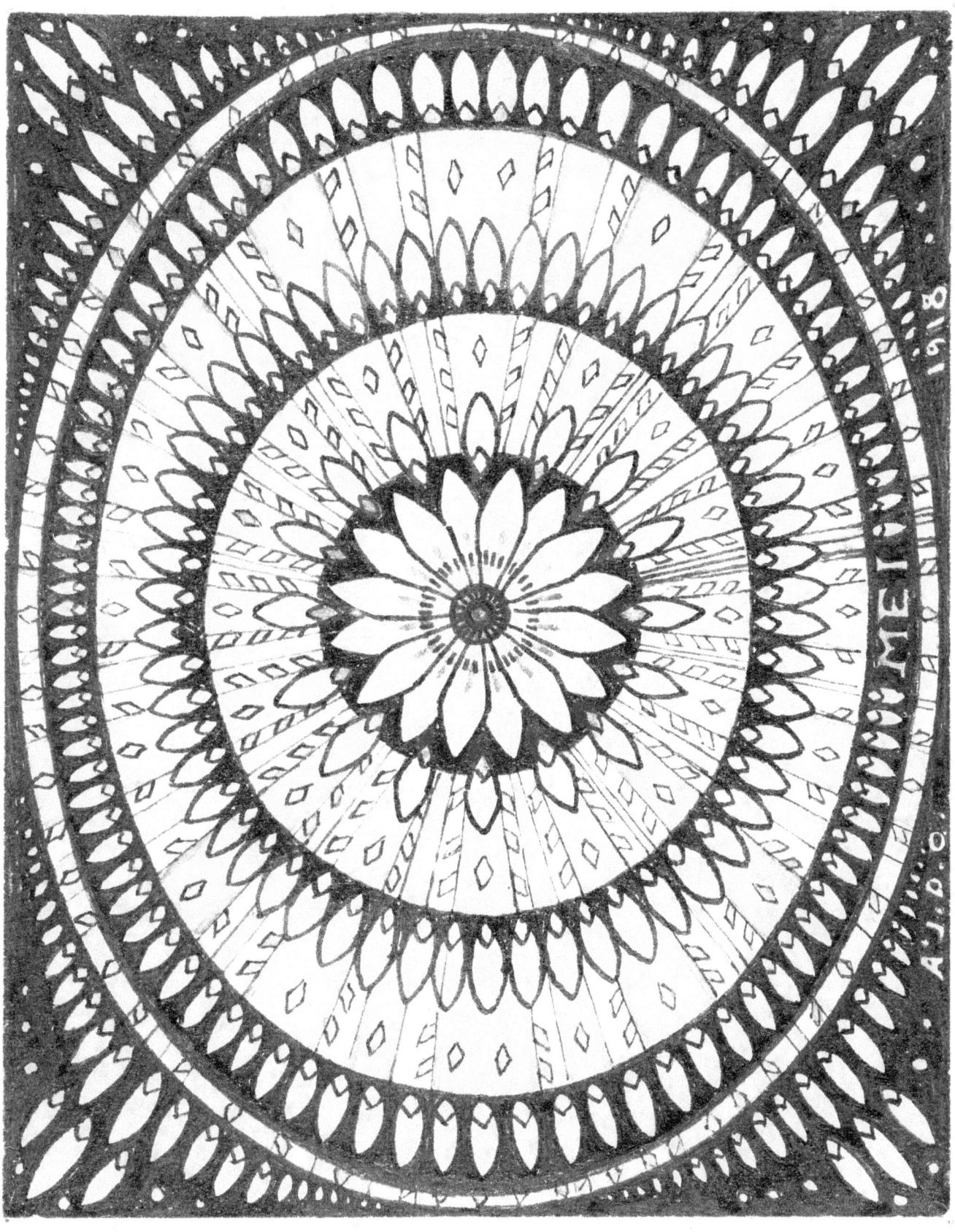

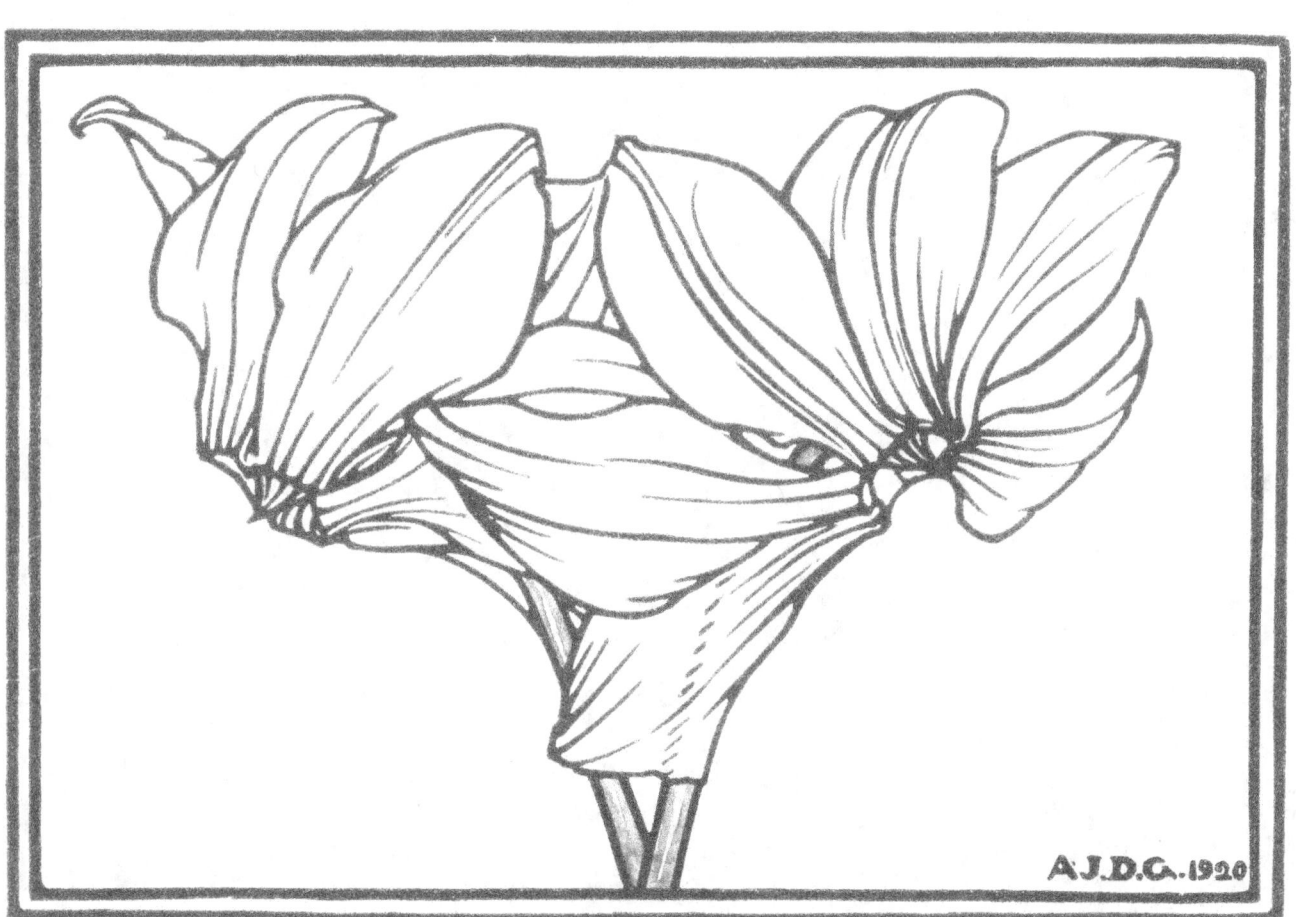

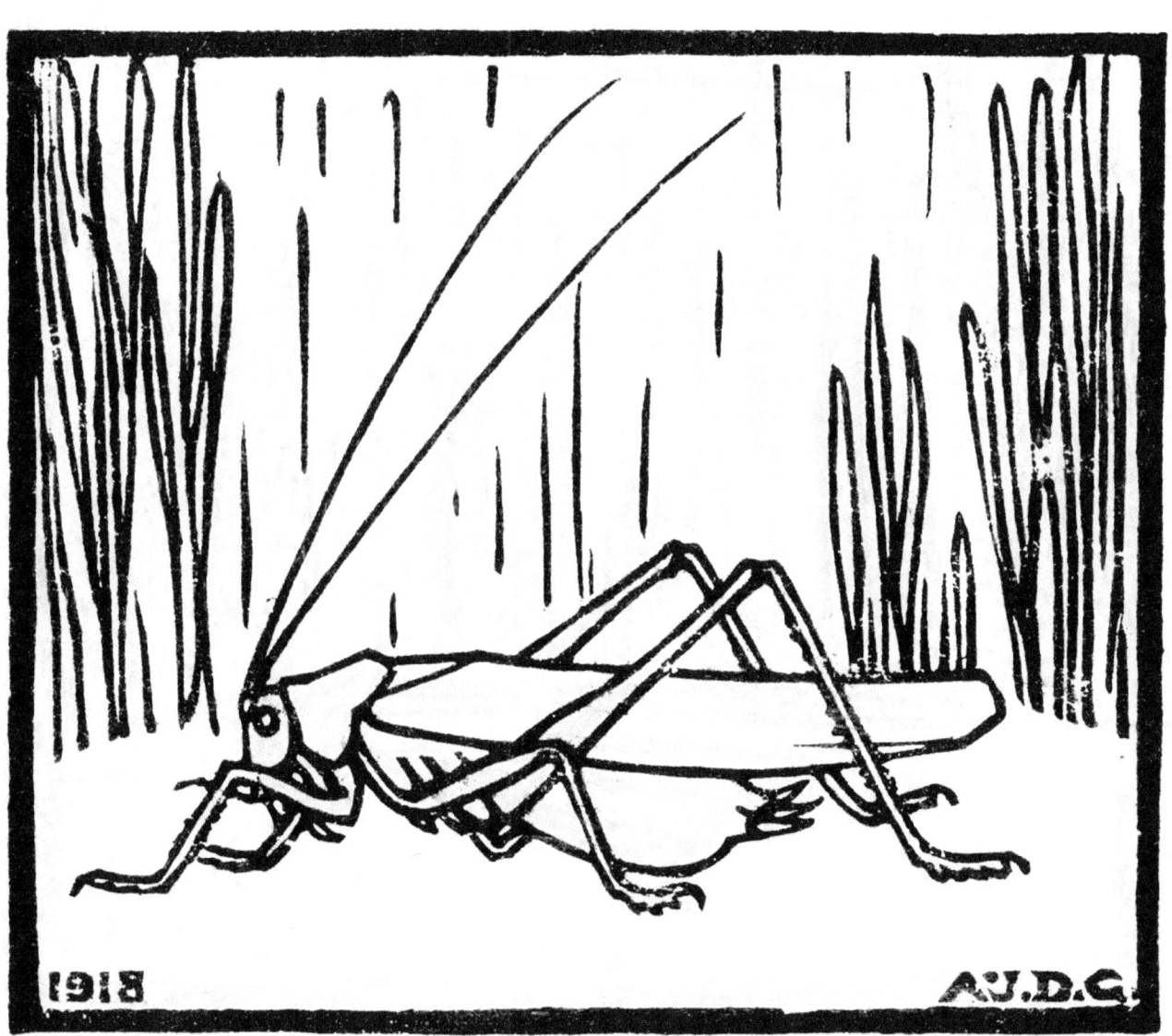

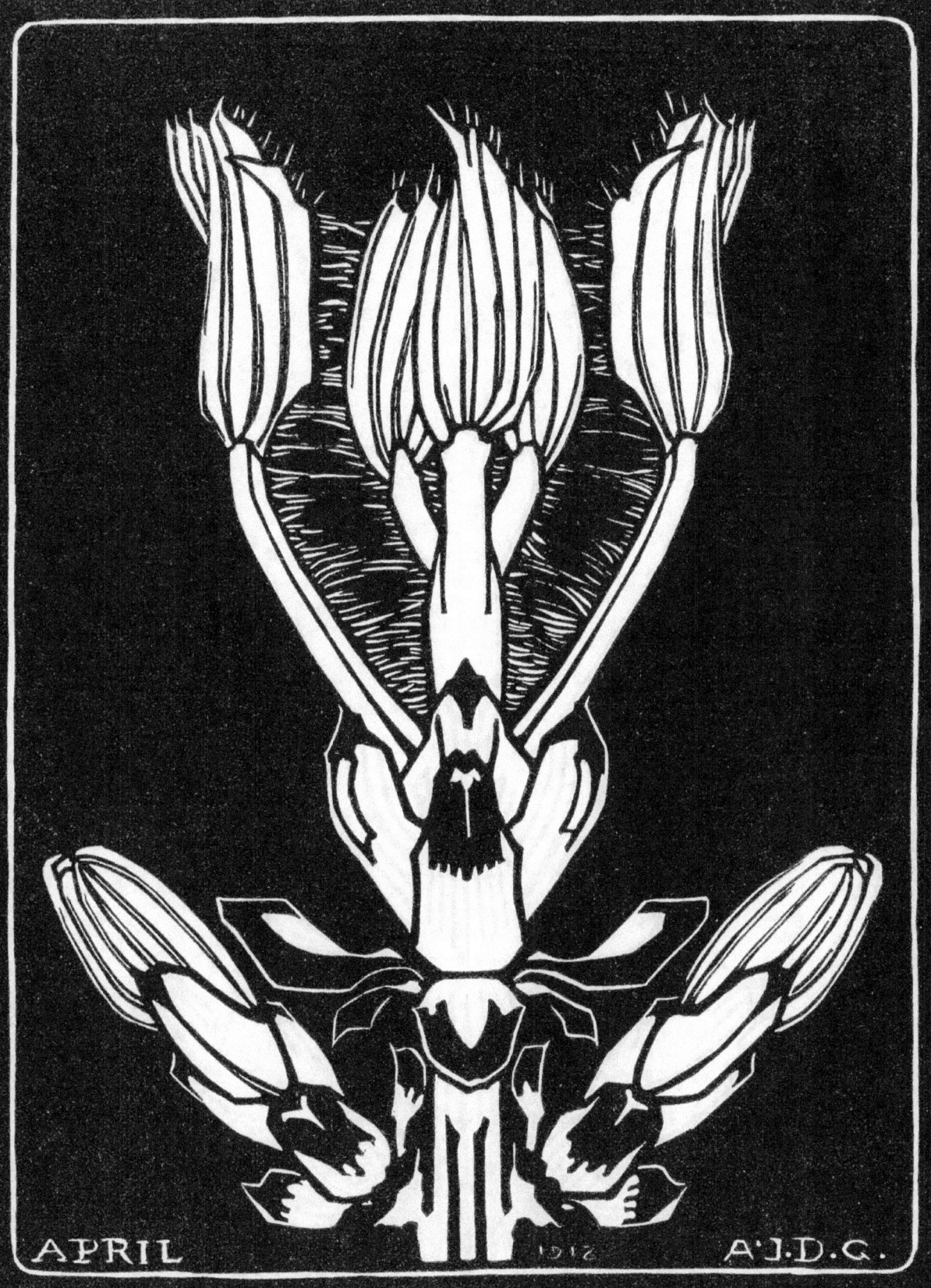

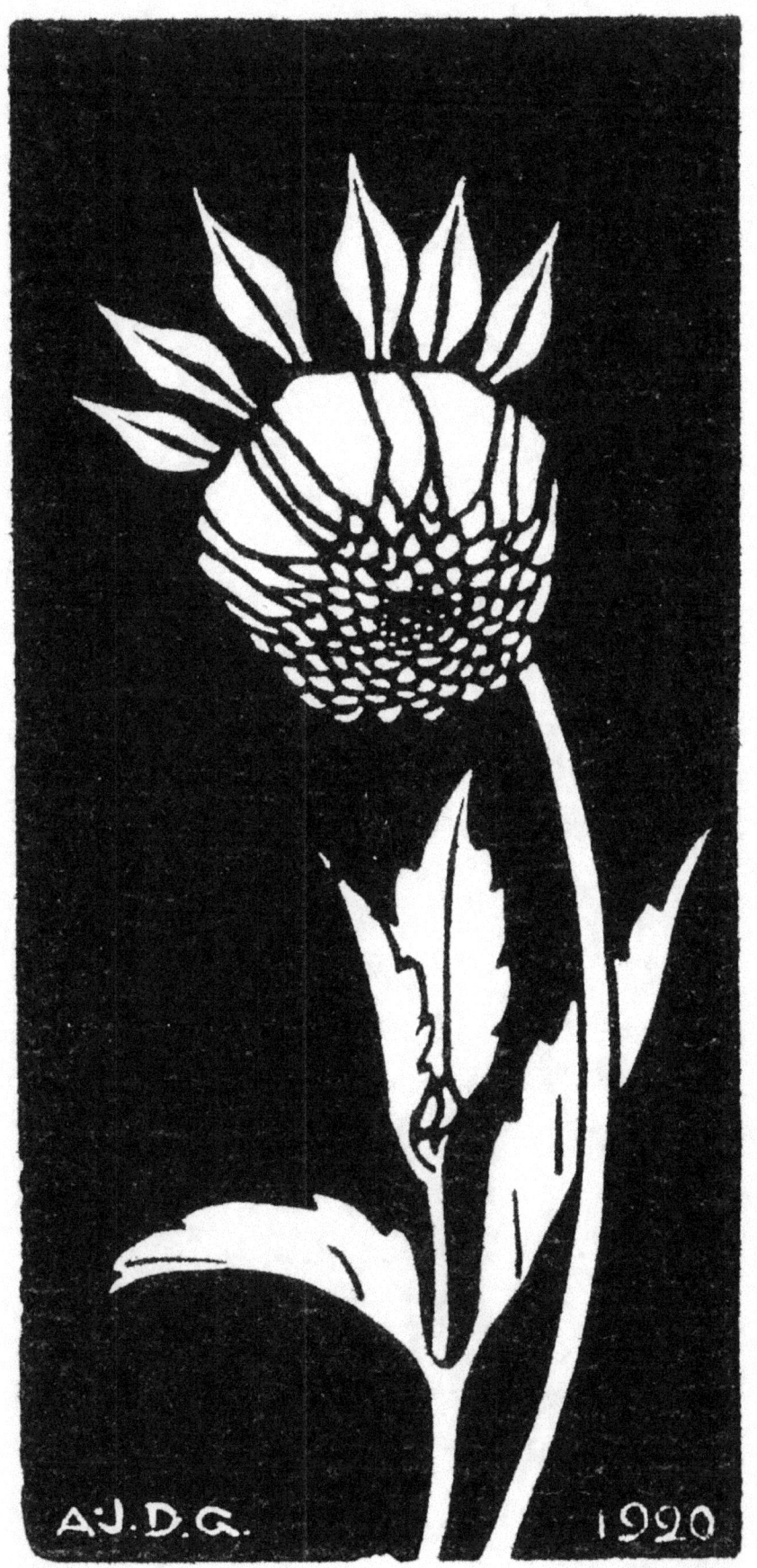

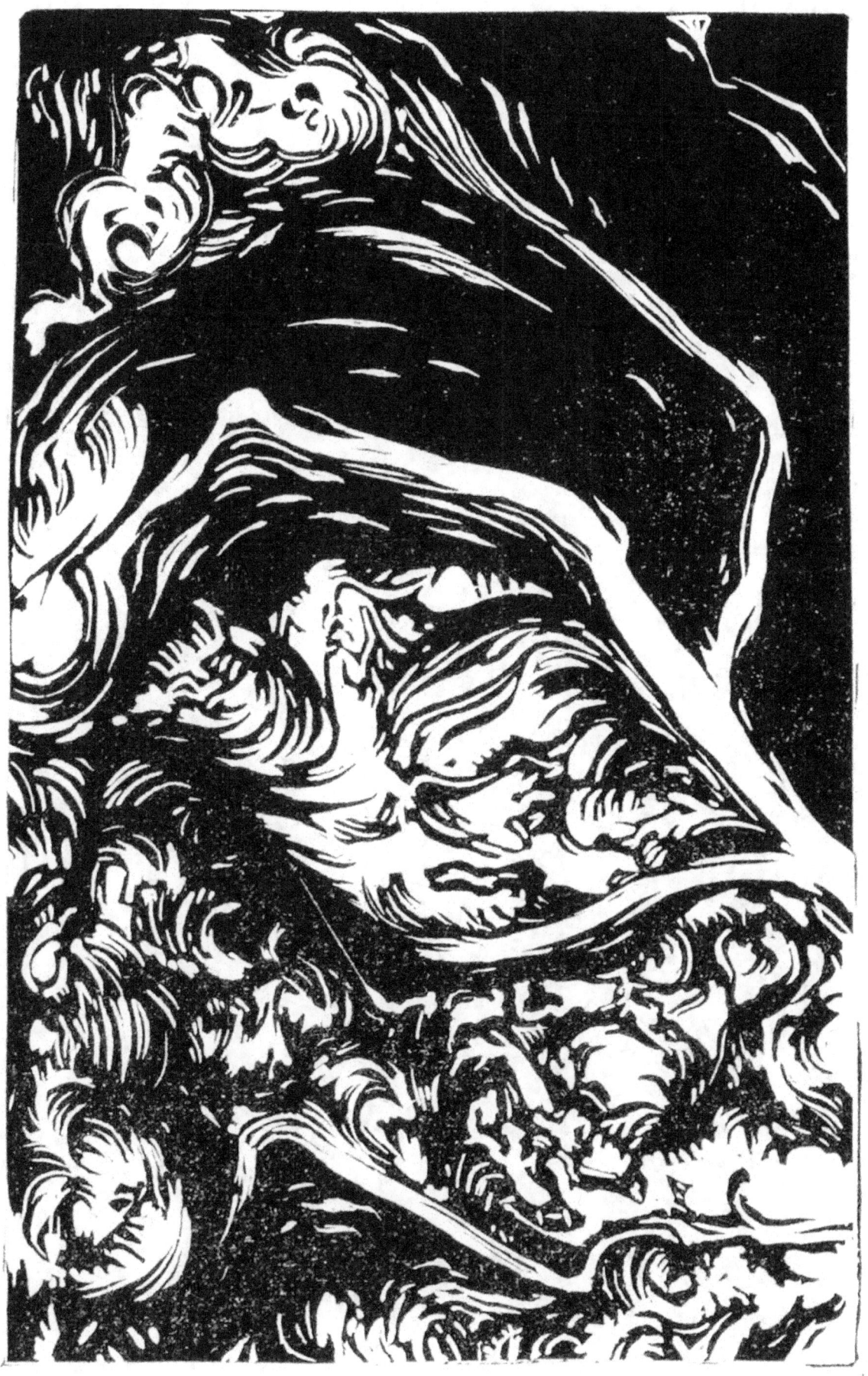

A.J. DEGRAAG.

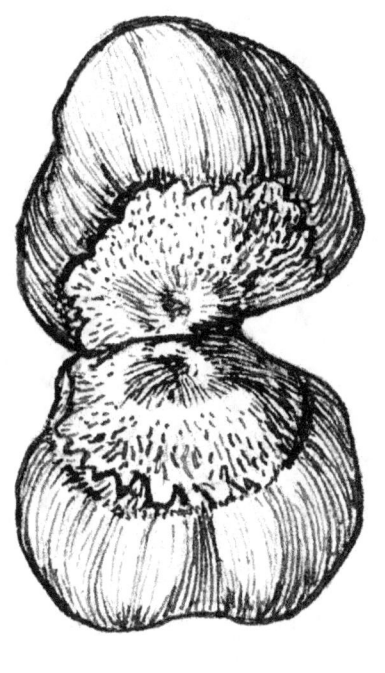

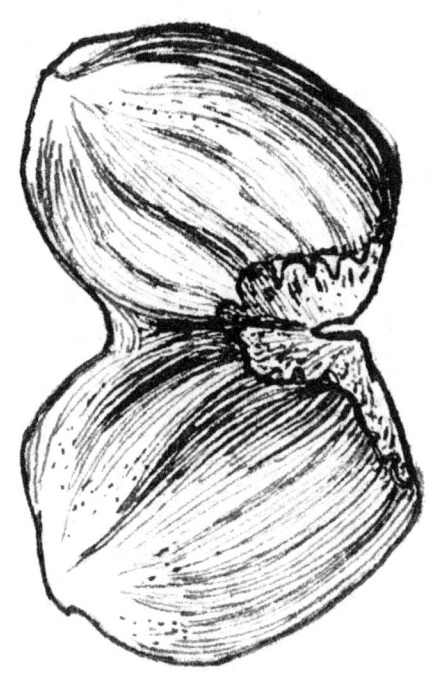

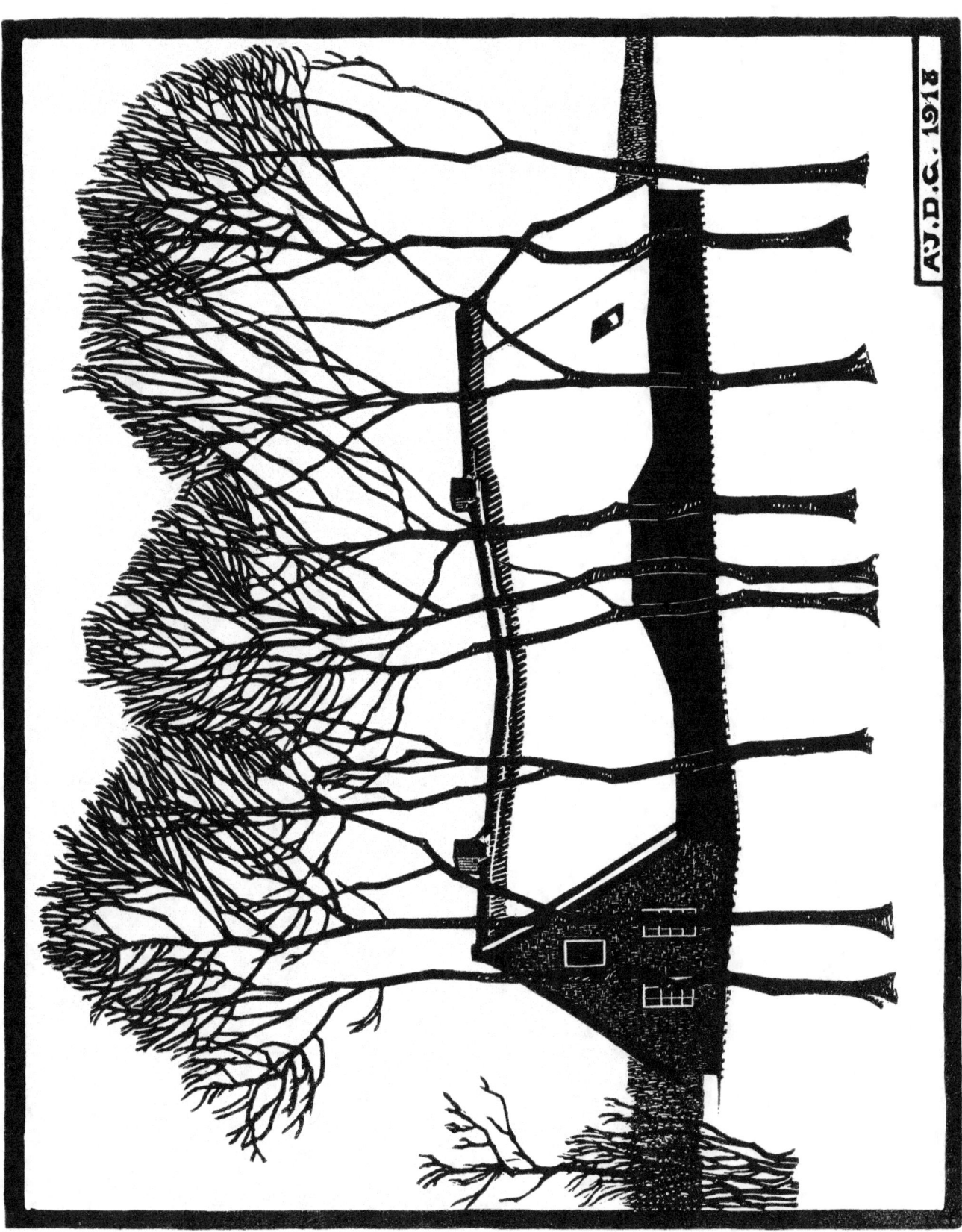

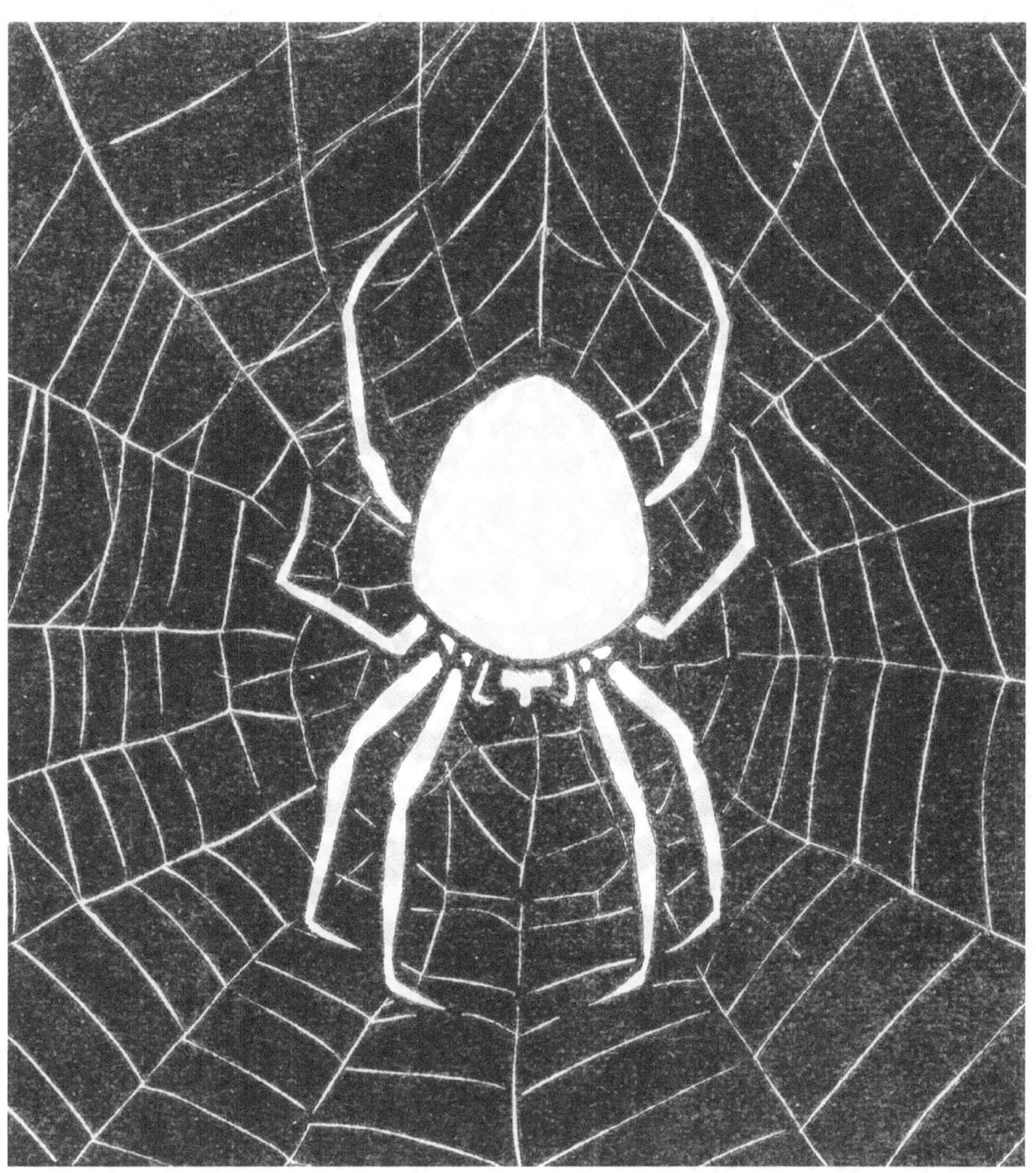

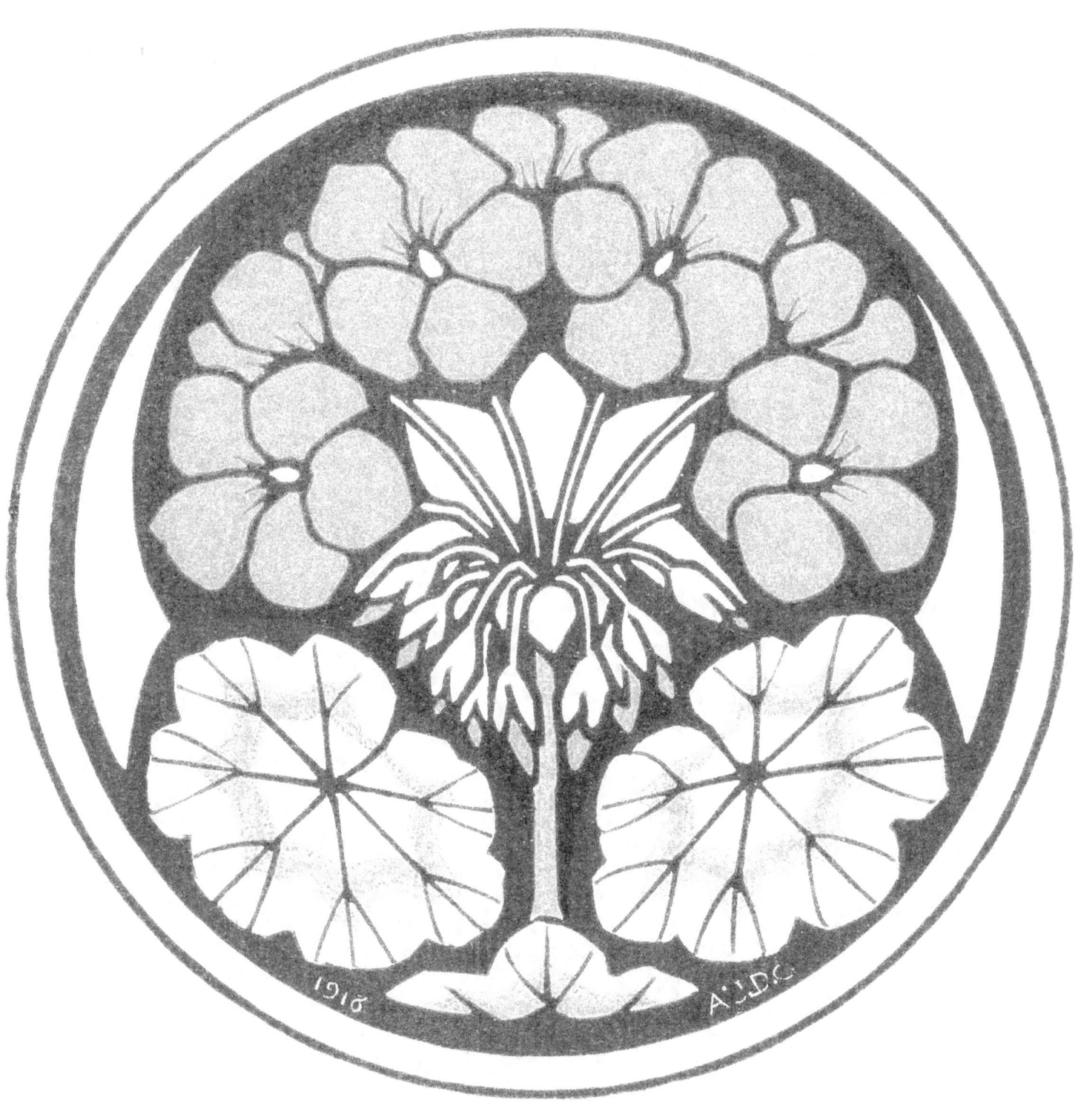

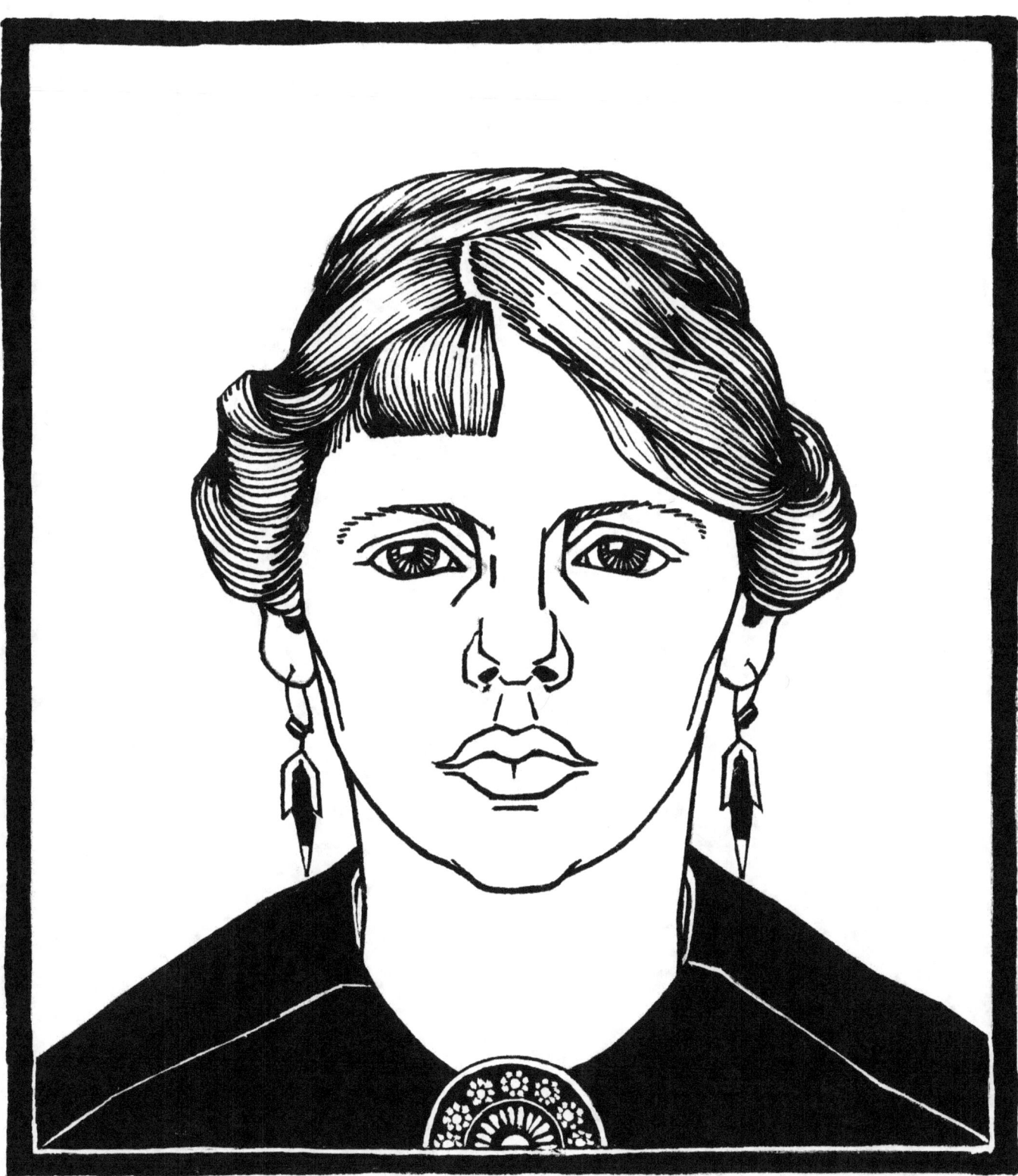

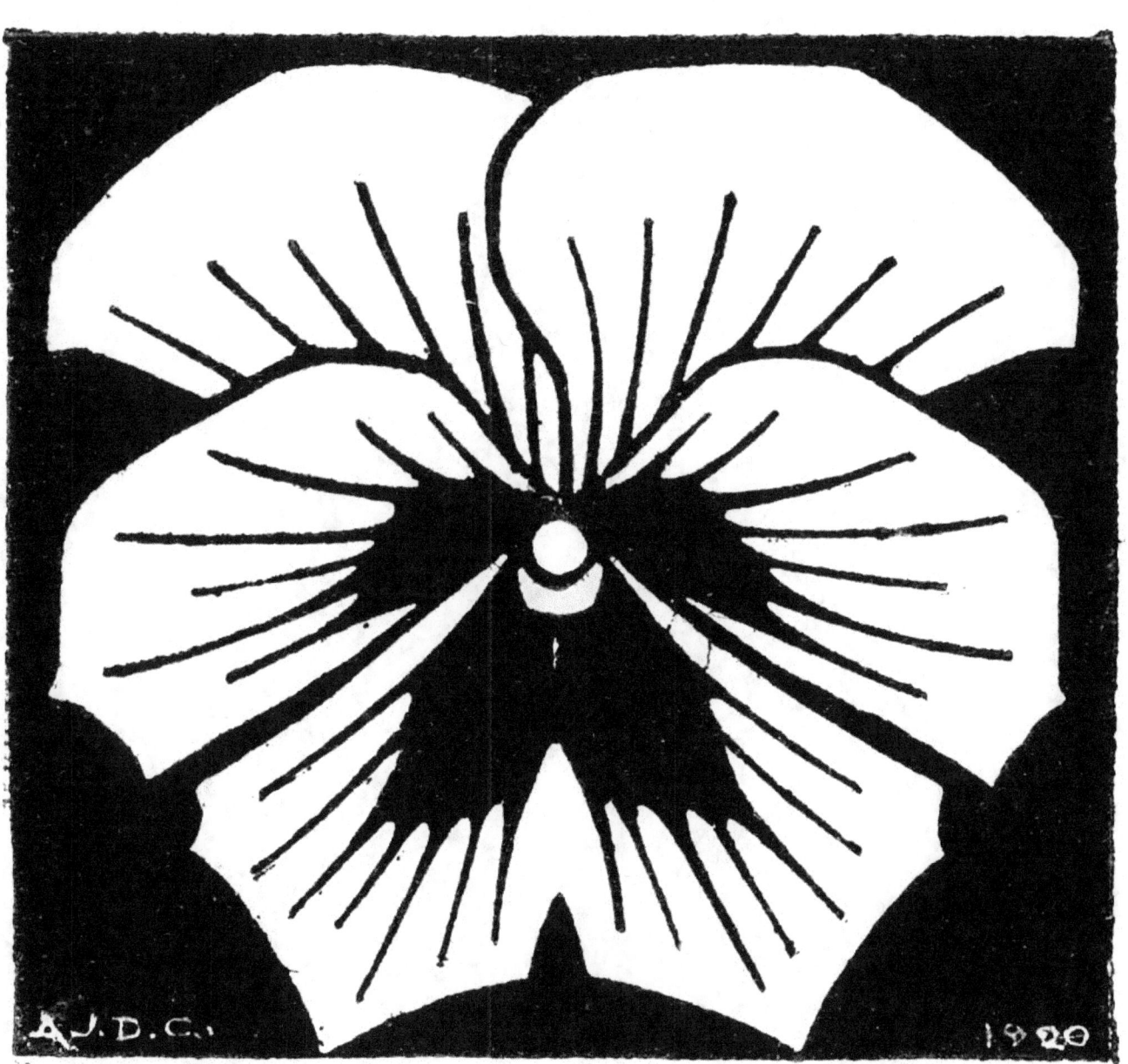

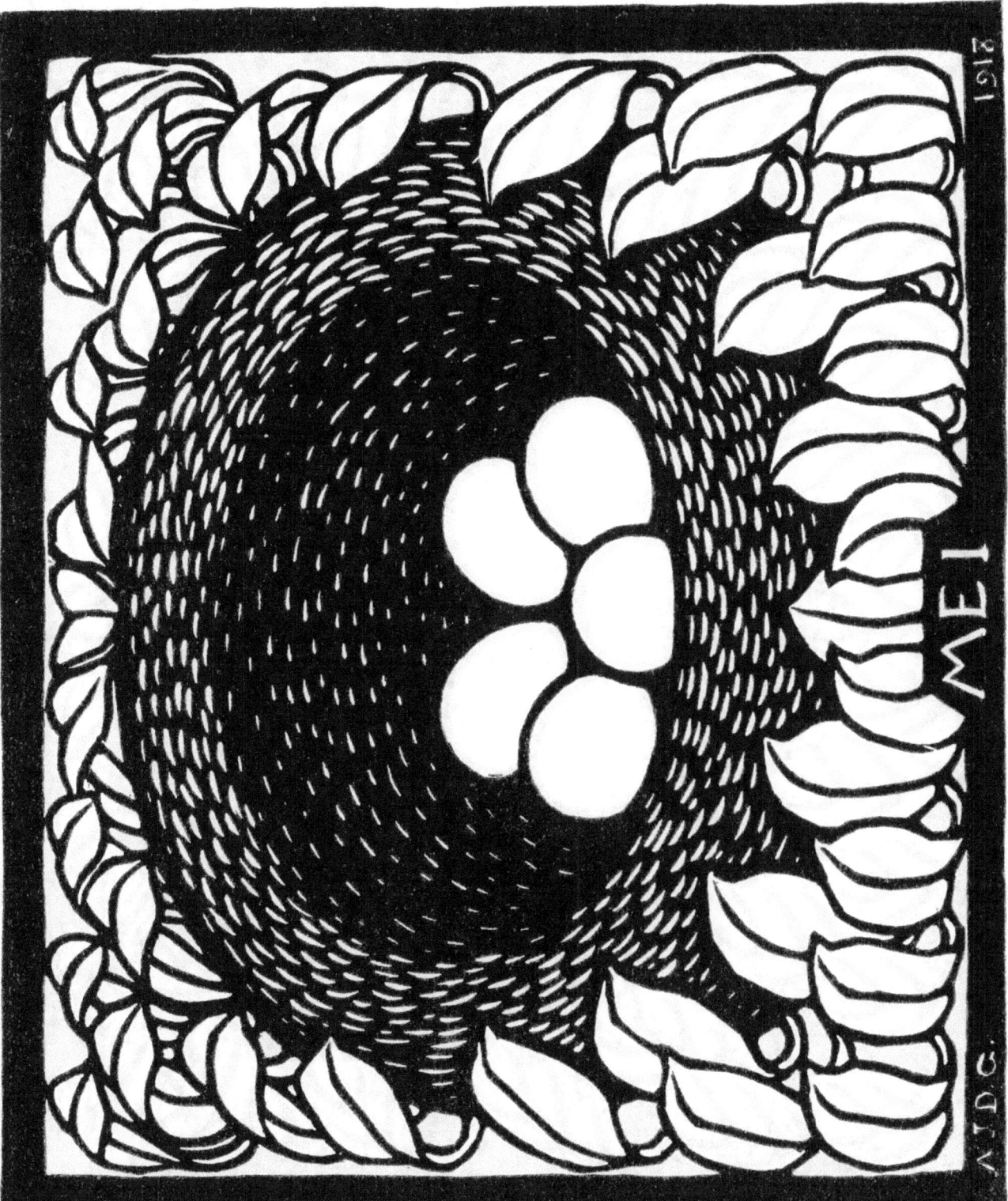

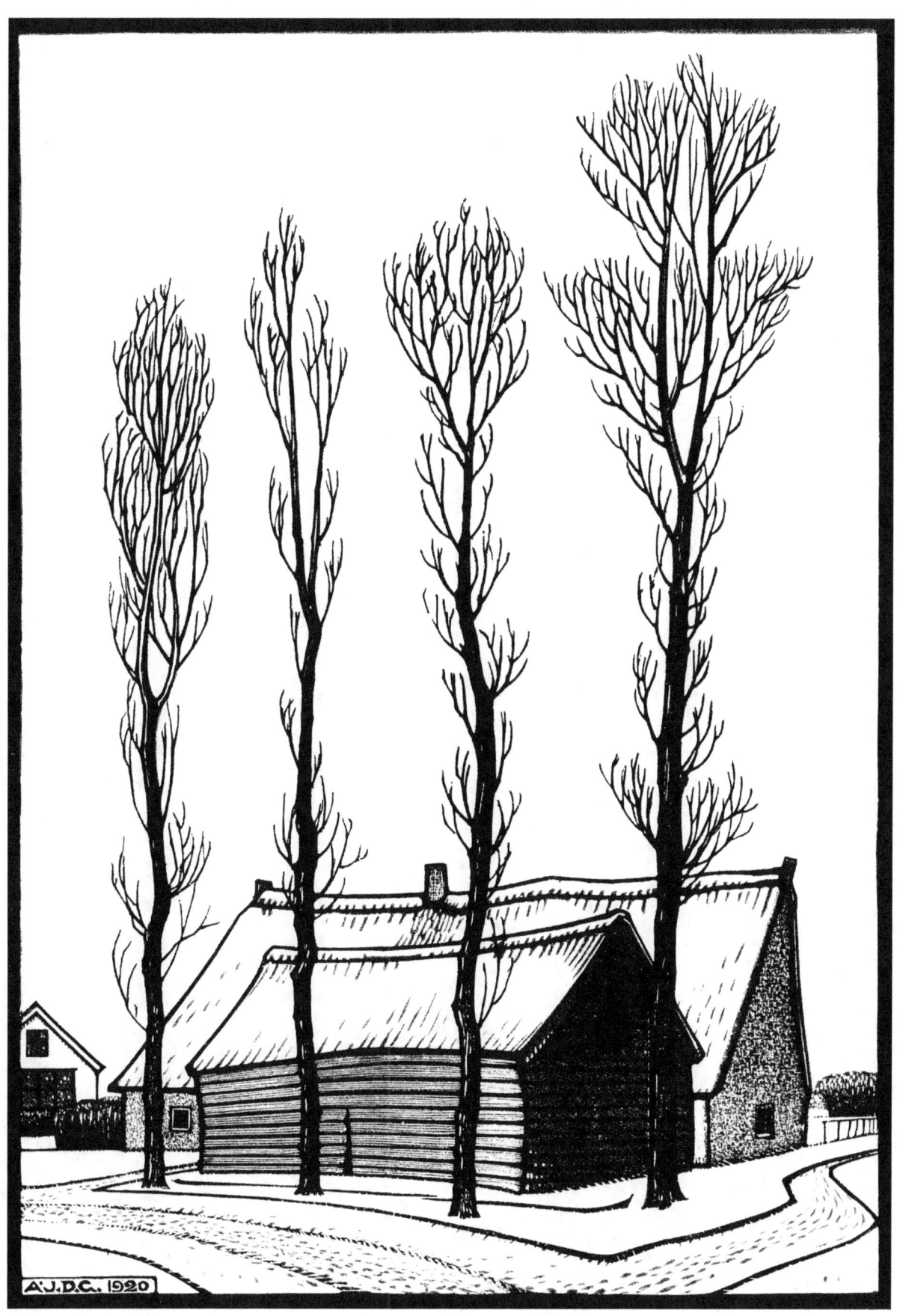

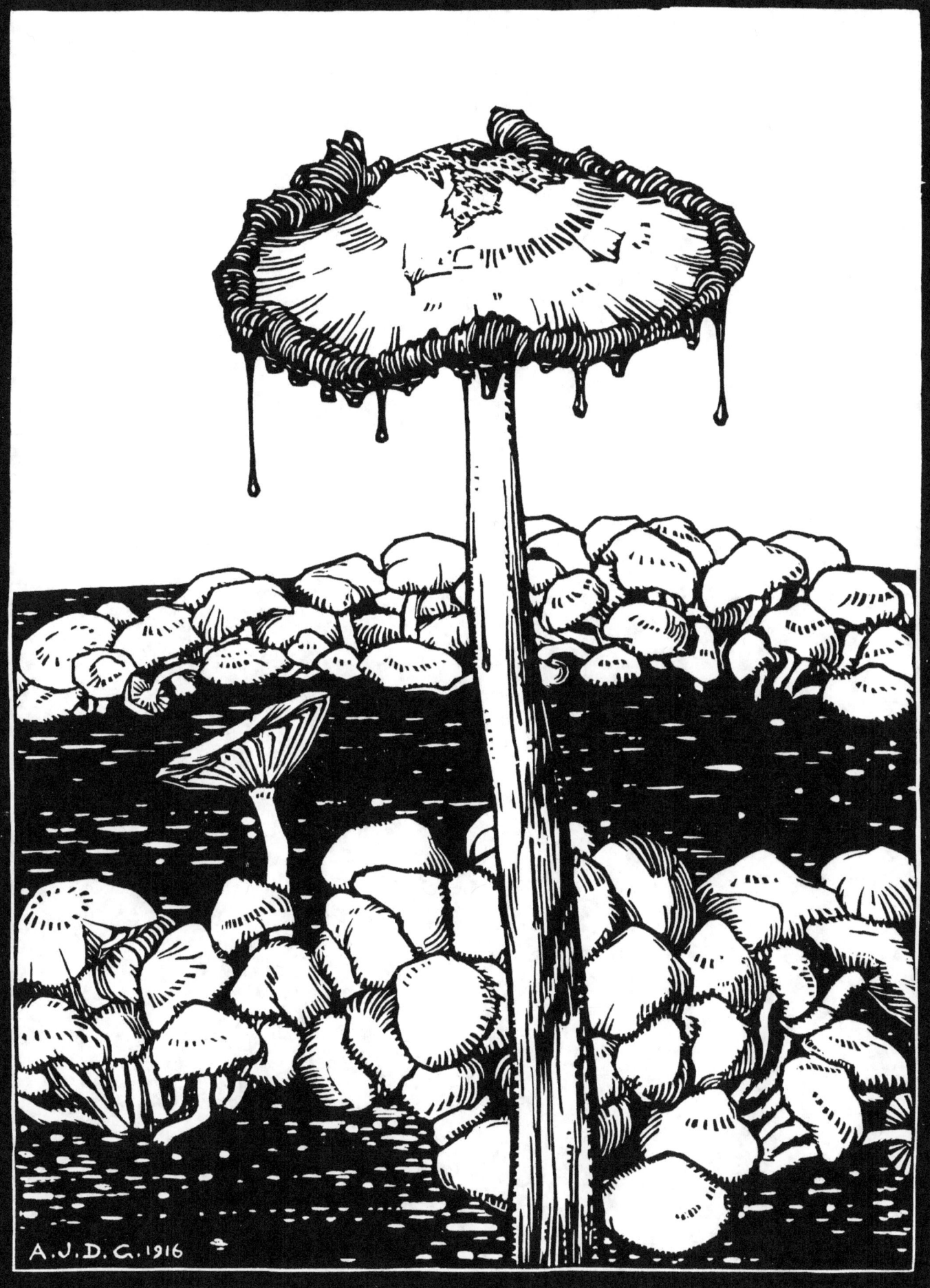

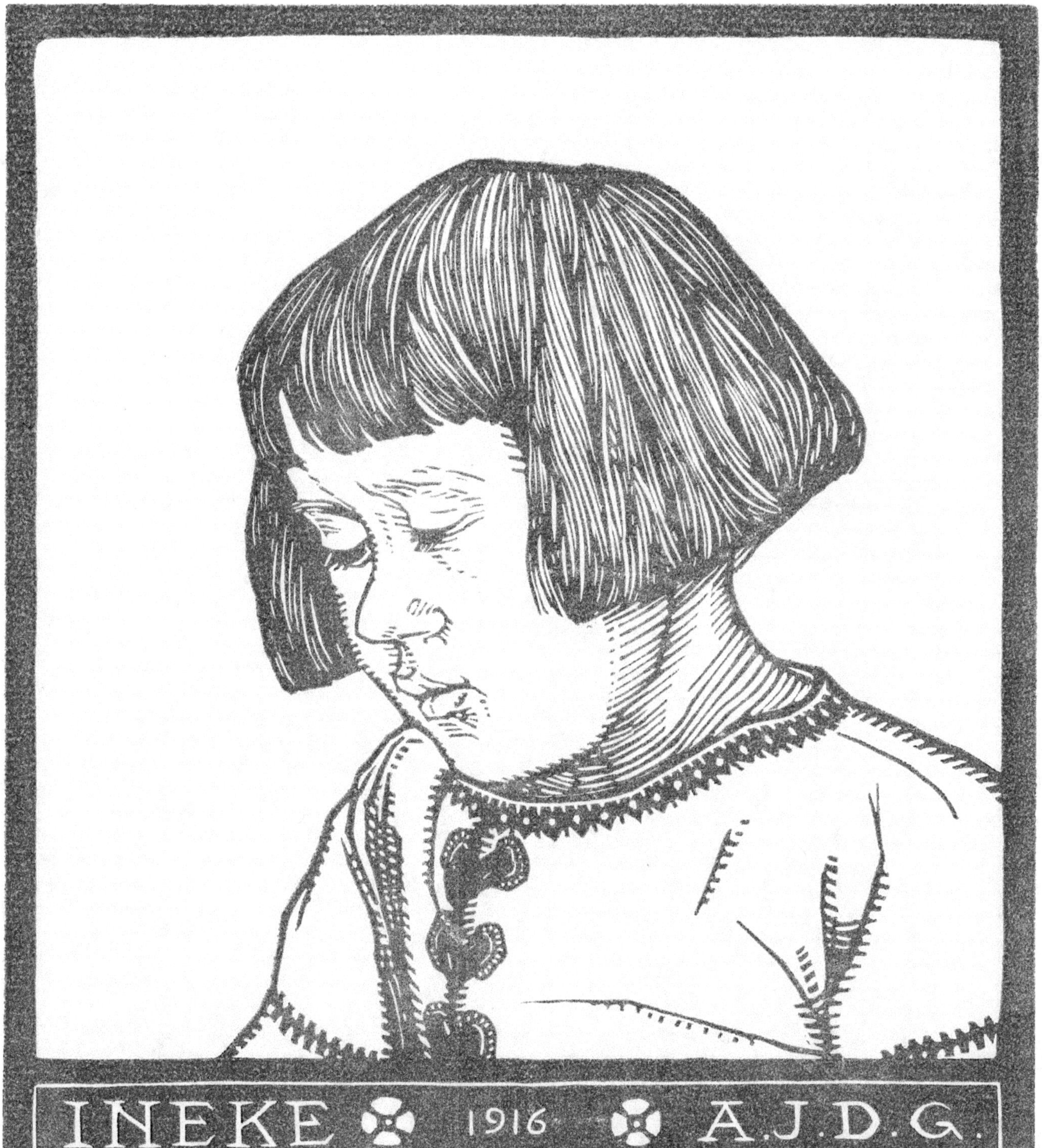

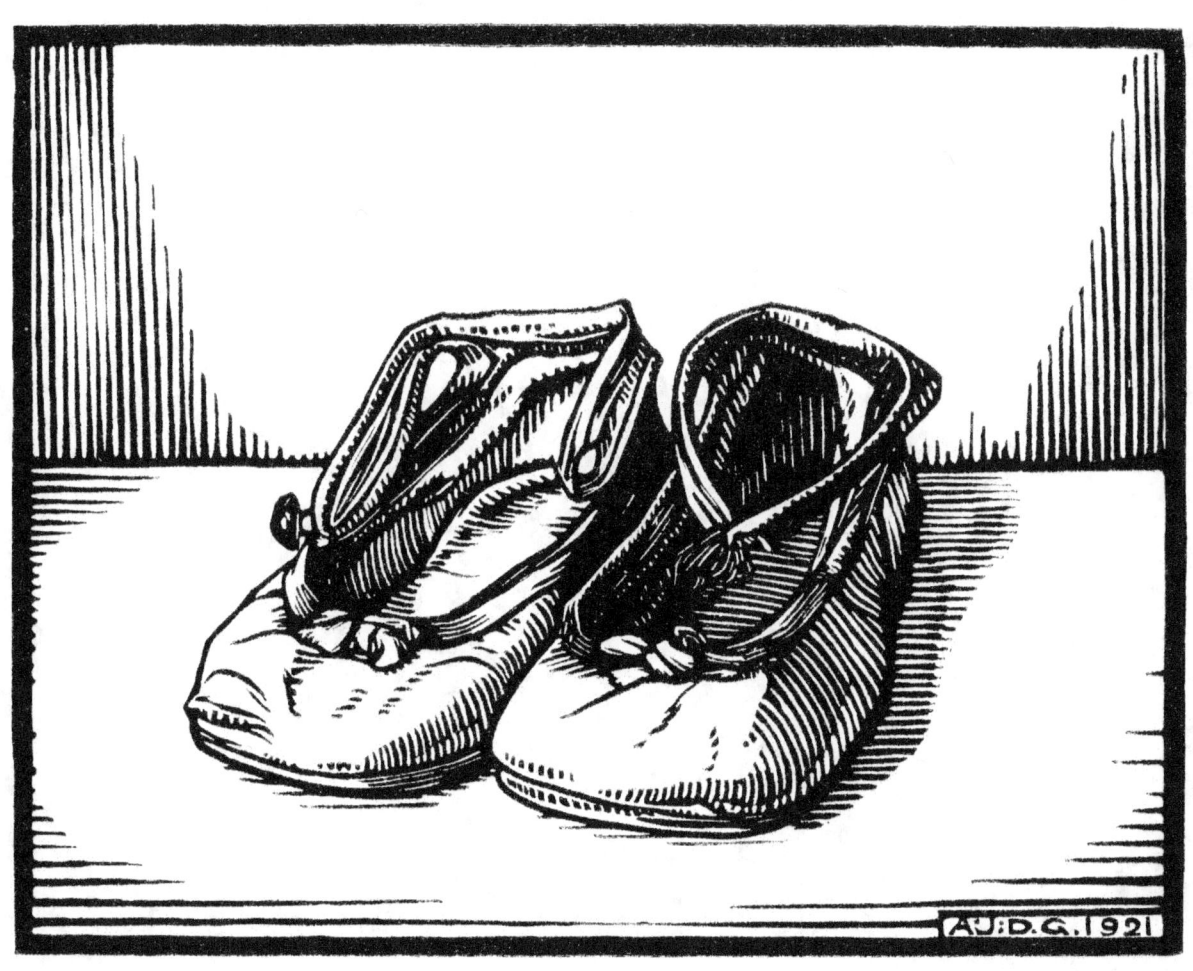

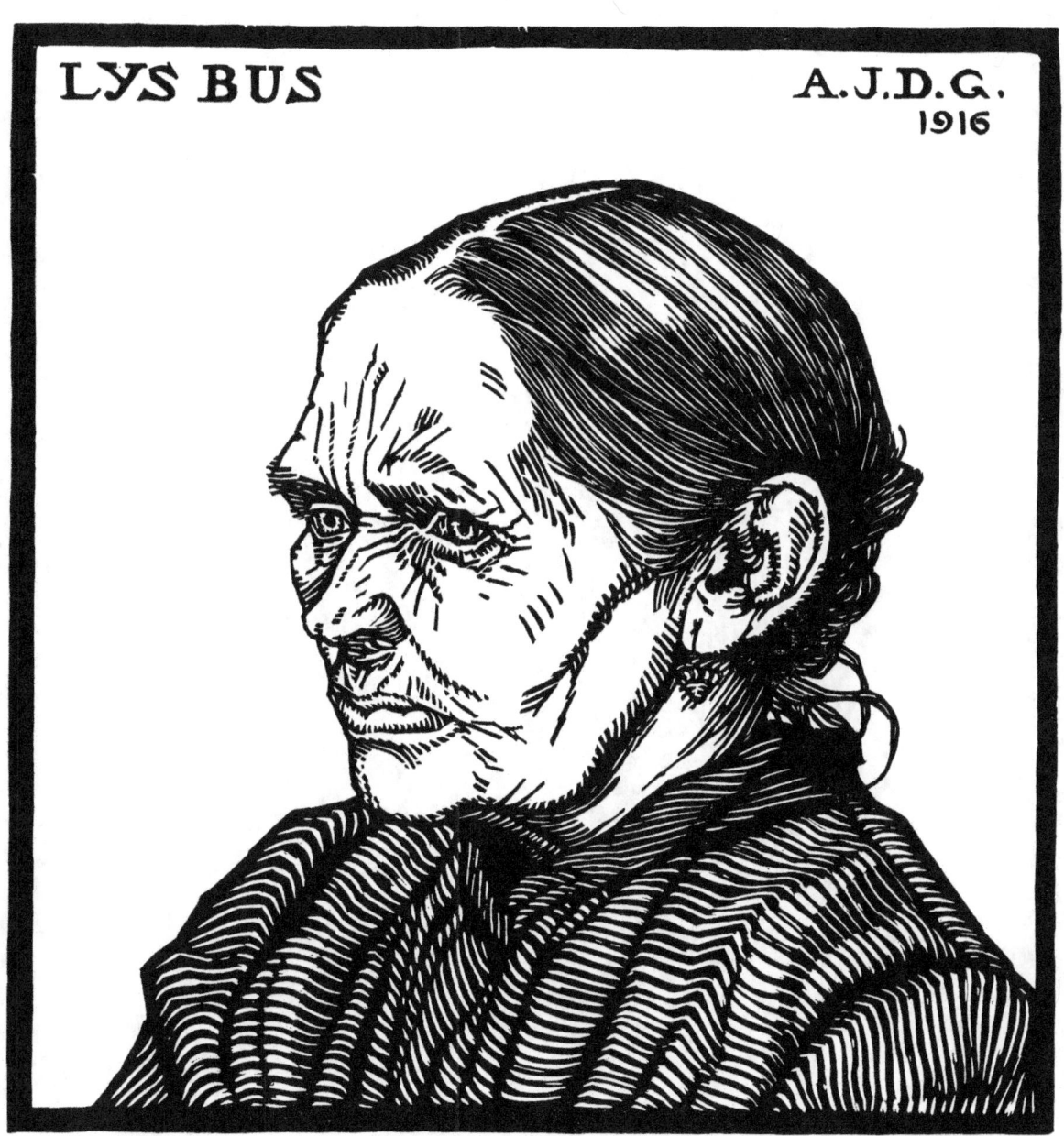

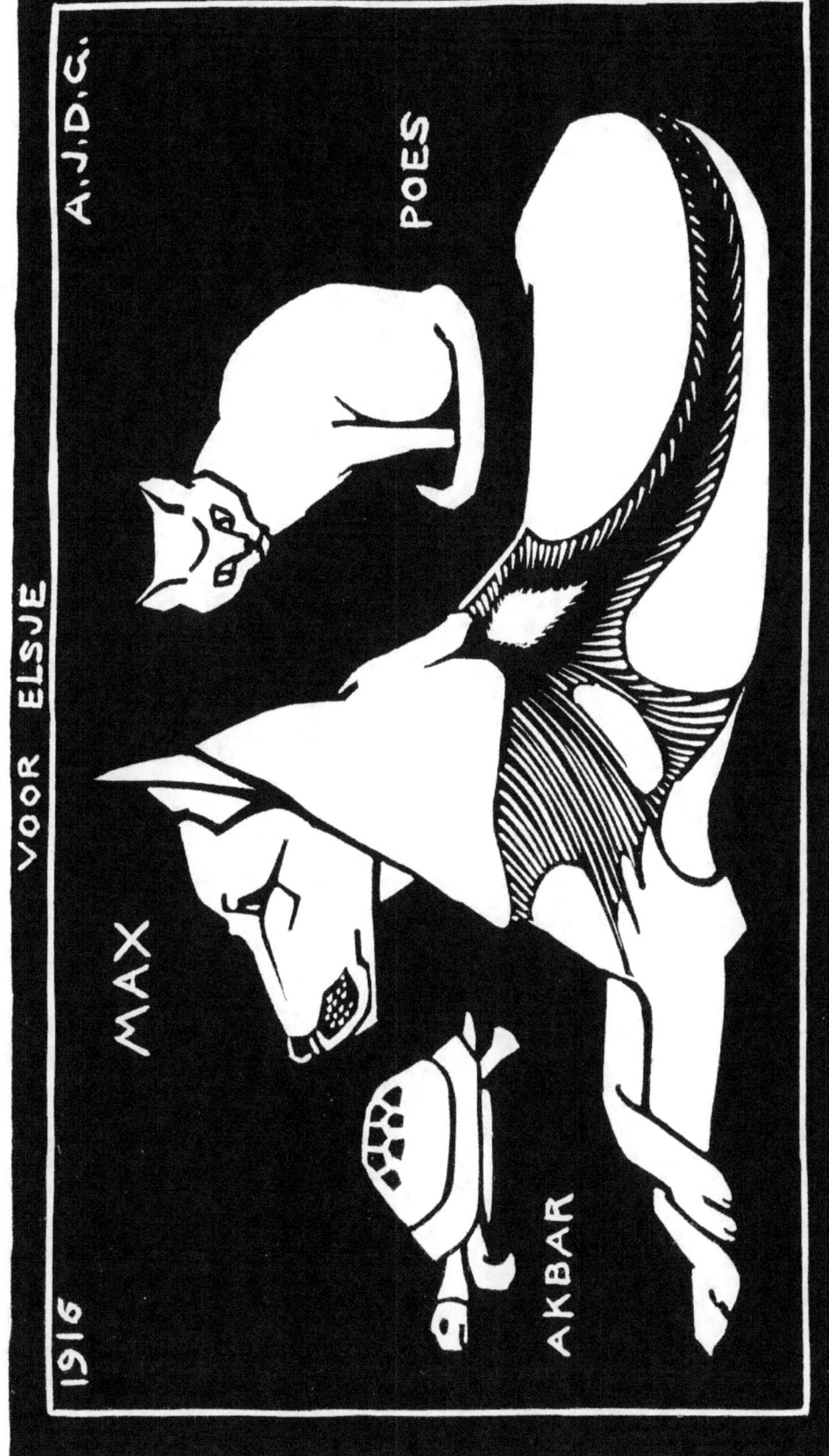

www.ingramcontent.com/pod-product-compliance
Lightning Source LLC
Chambersburg PA
CBHW082115220526
45472CB00009B/2187